'In your breath, I will find you.
In your prayer, I will answer you.
In your devotion, I will accompany you.'

Sister Miriam.

Intuition is the link between wisdom
and higher consciousness.

Ra, (the Sun God), Aten Temple, Egypt.

What people are saying

Peace between Breaths' is both an inspiration and invitation. Meditation teacher and spirit healer Feroze Dada takes us on a journey towards wisdom, through a dialogue of revelation between a spirit guide he encounters at the Sylvan Healing Sanctuary and Lily who is a metaphor for all of our struggles and stumbles in life, the sadness and the joy, the suffering and the awakening - all the mystery and the magic of what it is to be human.

The wisdom teachings that are revealed to Lily are underscored by a meditation practice and affirmations that ensure we engage with each and every encounter on the path we travel towards awakening. As readers, we come to understand that Compassion, Kindness and Positivity are prerequisites to finding tranquillity, that Meditation brings inner peace and awakened awareness, and we discover the connectivity of our souls through time and space. All of this helps us to direct our energies towards hope and promise.

Lily's story is our story, and inspires us to be attuned to the Spirit guides that are always with us, the healing for body and mind that we can easily reach for, and the gifts we already have that we can share with others as we learn to live life more fully and awaken to radiance.

Remember the Sanskrit proverb 'If you breathe well, you will live long on Earth' And read 'Peace between Breaths' in order to understand how to make the most of living your life.

Duncan Baird.
Publisher & Author.

'Peace between Breaths' is an antidote to the pervading sense of misery in which our world is currently mired. Dada's latest book is gently passionate in its celebration of the potential for each individual to lead a better life and contribute to a better world. It radiates optimism, not by denying or ignoring suffering and fear but by explaining how, through guided meditation, individuals can overcome fear and alleviate suffering by accessing and then celebrating their capacity for love, generosity, compassion and humility.

Its teachings go to the heart of what makes us human.

Sir Nigel Carrington.

'Peace between Breaths' is one of the most beautiful artistic books of the thousands of metaphysical books I have read in the last thirty years.

With his newest book Feroze brings Heaven to Earth through channelled messages from Sister Miriam and Joan, a spiritual teacher, healer, and medium in Spirit, allowing personal inner growth for those who absorb the vibration and energy of divine compassion from their inspired poetic words and picturesque images in a truly comforting and miraculous story of faith and courage.

A beautiful book of hope for a troubled world, with solutions through self-awareness of the Oneness of life, to heal a fractured physical reality. 'Peace between Breaths' holds the energetic force needed to connect to spiritual wisdom through guided meditations, silence, breath, intuition, an opening of hearts to soul presence, kindness, and a way to love with purpose.

A truly inspirational story about the infinite journey of a soul. 'Peace between Breaths' is a precious book to hold in your hands and heart forever.

Sheryl I. Glick.
Medium & Author.
Podcast Host: Healing from Within.

This is a truly inspiring book from the get-go. For those who know of Feroze's writings, this is a further step up and beyond his previous books. One has the sense of the 'Ladder of Divine Ascent' in these his latest writings. The ancient Celts had the concept of the 'thin place' geographically, where one feels closer to God. This makes for a powerful chemistry when mixed with deep meditative and prayerful practises. These combine to allow transcendental experiences.

This lovely inspirational book leads one to many thin places and introduces practices with great power to heal both the mind, body and soul. "The peace was a shell without the slightest fracture. I remained transfixed by its influence, then I felt I was whispering: "Come and see…" (George Seferis).

That is what you should do with this great book, come and see, much inspiration will come.

Professor J Richard Smith.
Surgeon & Writer.

If you are a meditation beginner or a spiritual old-timer, 'Peace between Breaths' offers something for everyone on their journeys of self-development. It was a privilege to edit Feroze Dada's latest book.

The channelled messages sent shivers of resonance through me with their inspirational missives of faith and strength alongside spine-tingling prophecies.

It is a book that offers hope to humanity - if we but only pause to take that breath, listen and take positive action. A must-read in the face of global economic, social and political unrest. Once again with his third book, Feroze has reminded us to focus on what is important in life.

Kate Delamere.
Author & Editor.

This is a time in human history when the world is becoming smaller as increasing connectivity brings humanity closer to a global culture of instant fulfilment. Such intense and widespread pursuit pushes the big questions that have eluded thinkers into the background.

Against this backdrop, weaving a narrative in the words of two spiritual guides, Dada explores the complex themes that shape and define our purpose and quality of life on this planet.

We all experience love, sadness, adversity, and hope, but have we realized the true potential of humility, vision, intuition, and wisdom?

He then shows the way to harness this potential within ourselves through various types of meditation, 'bringing peace to a troubled mind and a wounded heart.'

'Peace between Breaths' is a deeply moving book for anyone confronting life's profound questions.

Khalid Awan.
Chairman, TCS.

In 'Peace between Breaths', Feroze has managed to weave several different elements of narrative and visuals into a book of deep meaning. Feroze's bright and colourful images, many taken in holy places, are a form of visual punctuation like colourful threads in a tapestry.

It's a very effective book that will inspire anyone who reads its deceptively simple text to 'move on up' from sadness into a space between breaths which is the root of all positivity.

Jill Furmanovsky.
Photographer.

We are in a time of self-discovery, learning our true purpose as spiritual beings. Despite always being guided, the real question is: do we truly listen to hear? We fear the unknown and the intangible.

We've made ourselves rigid and linear, drowning in noise, unable to hear the wisdom guiding us. We need guidance in the world right now, and this book on the human spirit's illumination and self-discovery is exactly that. It reveals that wisdom has always been there, waiting for us to be still enough to feel and hear it. This is a timely discovery of life itself.

I highly recommend reading this book. It will change your life by opening the mind, heart, and soul to a higher consciousness.

Sara Troy
Self Discovery Wisdom.com

Dedication.

For my ever joyful first grandchild Layla Collins, born on 11 February 2019, and my second grandchild Rafferty Collins, newcomer to this earth plane on 19 December 2023.

Wishing you both a life of peace and love.

☙

In memory of Sister Miriam and Joan Fountain, whose lives on Earth and wisdom in Spirit, inspired this book.

☙

True beauty is in the eye of the beholder of wisdom.

Island of Hydra, Greece.

Preface.

My spiritual journey began when some 15 years ago I went to Myanmar to visit my wife's family. On a chance encounter, I became deeply involved in working with a Buddhist monastery in Shan Province where the monks taught me meditation.

At the same time with the guidance and wisdom of my Sufi teacher, Ustād, I set out on my spiritual journey, experiencing what it means to live a fulfilled and meaningful life.

A decade or so ago I began serving at the Sylvan Healing Sanctuary in London, teaching and promoting meditation. This is a community of healers, teachers and practitioners who offer energy healing, meditation and mindfulness.

When my colleague Michelle Spencer at The Sylvan Healing Sanctuary shared channelled messages from her spirit guide Sister Miriam, I was moved by the profound wisdom they contained.

Sister Miriam contacted her during circle meetings where inner members of the Sanctuary met for meditation and spiritual guidance in 2019. Later, during COVID times when we were unable to meet in person, Michelle continued to channel the messages at home and wrote them down to share with us.

Sister Miriam told her that in her last incarnation, she was a nun in the religious order of St Christopher 120 years ago in Ireland where she cared for children, going on to work with youngsters in the spirit domain after she passed.

Each message had encouragement and guidance for us to continue our work of healing and meditation at the Sanctuary. Later I reflected on them and discovered deeper insights. Each word resonated with the energy of truth in my heart. I intuitively knew the knowledge they carried was integrated in my soul and I felt called to share them with a wider audience.

To ensure the integrity of Sister Miriam's words, (and those channelled by medium Joan Fountain), they are in *italics* throughout this book.

At about that time my first granddaughter, Layla, was born on 19 February 2019, bringing joy to our family. And yet she had entered a world that was in turmoil with wars and conflict breaking out across the globe. I found myself wondering how I as her grandfather could share some of the wisdom from my spiritual teachers to give her a legacy that she and other new souls could learn from to live compassionately and in peace with each other.

One day while I was meditating at the Sanctuary, an idea came to me that I could share the uplifting and enlightening wisdom of Sister Miriam's messages in an inspirational story about the infinite journey of a soul.

The words would sit alongside photographs I'd taken on my spiritual pilgrimages and meditation retreats around the world; such as The Giza Pyramid complex in Egypt, Jerusalem, Inle Lake in Myanmar and La Verna and Assisi in Italy that were once the homes of St Francis of Assisi, an Italian mystic and Catholic friar, who founded the religious order of the Franciscans.

Each one of the topics on which Sister Miriam speaks stands alone to be meditated on as well as connected to the story to guide you as you navigate your way through life.

My deepest wish for you is to realise your potential, enjoy the gift of life and find peace of mind.

Feroze Dada.

ॐ

ಳಿ

"One day while I was meditating at
the Sanctuary, an idea came to me
that I could share the uplifting and
enlightening wisdom of Sister Miriam's
messages in an inspirational story about
the infinite journey of a soul."

Feroze Dada

ಳಿ

Peace between Breaths

Meditations for the Heart & Mind

by Feroze Dada

With

Messages from spirit guides

Sister Miriam

(Channelled by Michelle Spencer)

and

(Messages Channelled by)

Joan Fountain

Story development and Editor

Kate Delamere

All author income from this edition is donated to

The Sylvan Charitable Trust no 286004

Published by
Filament Publishing Ltd
14, Croydon Road, Beddington
Croydon, Surrey CR0 4PA

+44(0) 20 8688 2598
www.filamentpublishing.com

Peace between Breaths by Feroze Dada
© 2024 Feroze Dada

ISBN 978-1-915465-42-9

Printed in the UK

Table of Contents

What people are saying   3
Dedication.   9
Preface.   11
Foreword.   21

1. SPIRITUAL ENCOUNTERS   25
Silence. • Inner Voice. • The Soul. • Spirit Guides.

2. YOUR PATH.   37
You are Guided. • Guided Meditation. • The Secret of
Life • Higher Consciousness.

3. LIFE ON EARTH.   51
Reincarnation. • Lake of Peace Meditation. • Ecstasy. •
Joan's Sanctuary.

4. YOUR SENSES.   65
Equality. • Awareness. • Mind Meditation.

5. FORM.   75
Heart. • Body. • Energy. • Aura.

6. RISE AND SHINE.   89
Blossom. • Sparkle. • Compassion. • Courage.

7. WISDOM.   101
Kindness. • Faith. • Light. •Truth.

8. ATTACHMENTS.   109
Vibrations. • Change. • Letting Go.

9. EMPATHY.   115
Understanding others. • Voice and Tone. • Good
deeds. • Simplicity.

10. EXPAND YOUR HEART.   125
Positivity. • Shine and Share. • Generosity. • Insight.

11. AWAKEN.   137
Turn Towards the Light. • Gratitude. • Acceptance
Know Yourself. • Luck.

12. REBIRTH.   147
Stay on the path. • Breathe. • Freedom. • Oneness.

13. ELEVATE YOURSELF.   155
Anchor. • Higher Self. • Peace. • In the Moment.

14. REALISATION.   163
Spring fever. • Consciousness.

15. JOAN'S HEALING.   167
School of Life. • Children. • Joy. • Golden Age. • Spirit
Aid.

16. JOAN'S SILVER LININGS.   177
Optimism. • Free Will. • Humility. • Vision.

17. LOVE.   185
Service. • Intuition. • Wisdom.

18. SWEET PARTINGS.   191

GUIDED MEDITATIONS AND AN AFFIRMATION. 196
Meditation Teaching. • Guided Meditation.•
Affirmation.

The Sylvan Charitable Trust number 286004   215

Acknowledgements.   216

About the Author.   217

అ

Room in The Rocca Maggiore Fortress in Assisi, Italy.

Foreword

Many things touch the soul that are great spiritual gifts. Music. Art. And words.

Words have always been an escape as well as a guide for me. They helped me make sense of the world when I no longer understood it and changed my perception of how I saw things.

They hold the power to express love, pain, grief, confusion, wisdom, knowledge, hope and empathy. They've been my friend when I was lonely and in the dark pit of despair. And comforted me during difficult times.

They allowed me to communicate privately through a sheet of paper when I could not express myself to another person. They moved me to tears and triggered emotional releases, as well as bringing peace to my troubled mind and wounded heart.

About ten years ago at the Sanctuary, spirit guide Sister Miriam made her presence known, to say that she wanted to use me to speak her words.

Her words were gentle and full of wisdom. She makes herself known to me as a presence on my right side and I sense her around me. I feel her and her vibration of peace and love.

For many years before I was aware of Spirit, I'd be guided by what I thought was my inner voice but now I realise it was her, guiding me, guiding me to go somewhere or try something.

At the beginning, my voice would crack as I tried to bring her messages through because I lacked confidence. When lockdown started the messages became stronger in the privacy of my home and I wrote them down to share with other healers and colleagues at the Sanctuary. Her messages became a way of bringing us together, as well as acknowledging that we were united in pain during this time but also bonded by hope.

We were lonely, craving to see and feel the embrace of loved ones. Shy and lacking self-confidence, Sister Miriam opened up a psychic gift that had remained dormant in me until then.

She became my constant companion. I'd feel her draw close, urging me to enter a quiet state and quieten the chatter of my mind. Her presence was impossible to ignore and my confidence grew as I spoke the words, she gave me. I'd hear her beautiful soft voice of comfort and encouragement in my ear telling me simple and universal truths. With her gentle reassuring presence, I channelled her words of peace and wisdom.

When my powerful ego got in the way, I'd block her wisdom and I gradually learned to step aside and trust in the process to let her words flow.

She's shown extraordinary patience, encouraging me to have faith, sit quietly and listen to her guidance.

I see her kindly smile in my mind's eye as she watches me struggle with doubt like a patient mother watching her child overcome difficulties at each stage of their life.

My faith in her is absolute compared to the wavering faith in myself. But with my beloved spirit guide at my side, I have no doubt I will improve.

When Feroze first asked if he could use her words of hope, love, compassion and truth in a story, I was thrilled. Her messages have been a constant source of love and support in my life, and I know they will be for readers too.

I'm grateful to him for sharing her wisdom in this wonderful and inspired tale that will bring delight and support to young and old alike.

Michelle Spencer.

Healer and Psychic.

❧

Sanctuary of St Francis of Assisi,
La Verna, Arezzo, Italy.

1. SPIRITUAL ENCOUNTERS.

Silence.

In your breath, I will find you.

As darkness fell, Lily sat in bowed silence in the medieval chapel at La Verna in Italy. She didn't smell the sweet scent of the calla lilies and white roses decorating the nave or see the beauty in the sacred icons in the stained-glass windows. Her mind was firmly imprisoned in the past.

The fingers of her hands were white with cold when the nun materialised in the stone doorway as if from thin air.

Dressed in a white tunic that swept the ground, she moved soundlessly toward her. From a distance, it appeared as if she was floating a few inches above the floor.

Her hands were hidden beneath the long flowing sleeves of her habit, pressed against her slender waist decorated with a simple belt of black woven wool. Her face was masked by a long black veil.

Lily stumbled to her feet. She didn't know how long she'd sat there; she'd lost track of time. Perhaps she was coming to tell her the chapel was closing?

Two wet trails ran down her cheeks, evidence of her grief, and embarrassed, she roughly rubbed away her tears.

'I'm sorry. What...?'

The nun raised a finger, urging her not to speak.

At first, she thought she heard the sound of the wind outside before realising the nun was saying her name.

Lily... Li...ly...Lil...ly...'

She knew her name! It meant fertility despite her childless life since the loss of her newborn child Ruby, a beautiful baby girl with emerald eyes and golden hair, ten years ago.

'I need to tell you...*Change cannot happen without upset and disturbance. It's vital you go inside, to a deep place of peace that rests within us.*'

Her words were like gentle caresses.

But Lily flinched as if she'd been struck. How did she know about her upset and disturbance? What could this stranger know about the sadness she carried? The sorrow she'd lived with for so long...

A familiar wave of suffocating black grief rolled across her chest, making her gasp. The day she gave birth to her child may have been a decade ago but the grief was as fresh as the day she'd held her for the first and only time in her arms.

Her heartache keeping her separated from the joys of the world. Her barren life a sorrow to bear.

How she ached to hold that tiny girl…willed her still heart to beat…

The nun was metres away now. Her face shielded behind her habit. A sense of urgency in her voice.

'I can give you knowledge to access a place of peace. A gift you can then share with others.'

'But who are you?' Lily's voice trembled. No one knew she returned each year to this place to remember her child whose life on Earth had been snatched away far too young.

'Sister Miriam.'

'How do you know my name?'

The nun laughed, sitting down next to her on the wooden pew.

'I know you well, I'm here to guide you.'

Lily frowned, puzzled.

The woman was so close she could make out her face, a grey shadow behind the lightweight cloth.

'I'm your spirit guide. Here to reveal to you the secrets of life on Earth.

Are you ready?'

Lily nodded slowly.

'Then I'll begin.

'Our breath holds the secret of birth, life and death on this earth plane. We take our first in-breath when we're born and the last out-breath when we leave.

'In between our first and last breaths lie the deepest secrets of life. Sit in meditation, be aware of the breath through your nostrils, going in and out. In the breath, you'll find the secrets of what you need, not what you want.'

Lily focused on her nostrils, the air tickling the end of her nose.

After what seemed like an eternity, Sister Miriam spoke again.

'Become aware of the pause between inhaling and exhaling. In that pause, allow yourself to enter the stillness where there's peace.

'Lose yourself in your inner world. Focus on your inner peace. In just a few moments, a shift in perception will take place.'

'The peace between your breaths is where we connect. It can offer you so many gifts.'

Lily looked away for a second. When she looked up the woman had vanished, leaving behind a musky scent of sweet roses, like an invisible trail of petals as the only proof she'd been there.

For the briefest, sweetest of moments, the iron hand of grief clamped around Lily's heart had gone and she felt calm, uplifted.

In the emptiness, she could have sworn she felt Sister Miriam's warm breath against her ear.

'In your breath, I will find you. In your prayer, I will answer you. In your devotion, I will accompany you.'

ॐ

'I need to tell you... Change cannot happen without upset and disturbance. It's vital you go inside, to a deep place of peace that rests within us.'

ॐ

Chapel at La Verna, Arezzo, Italy.

Inner Voice.

Listen to the voice of peace and stillness.

L ily sat on in silence in the chapel, trying to process what had happened.

Somewhere deep inside her, a small voice struggled to speak. With every fibre of her being, she strained to hear…

'When we sit in silence in meditation, we hear the voice of truth. It is undiluted by the noise of our thoughts and unedited by our pre-conditioned mind. There, we receive pure inspiration.' And suddenly Lily knew this voice had been there all along but she hadn't been listening. It was someone who had her back.

A perfumed scent of roses drifted through the air.

'Your soul needs quiet to be heard.'

Sister Miriam's voice was as clear as crystal. *'Peace, quiet and calm.*

'Find time every day for not doing. Not thinking, wishing or complaining. Your being will swell with peace and love.'

'Listen to that voice within. It has many invisible gifts for you.'

Castello Monteriggioni, Siena, Italy.

The Soul.

Travel to your heart from your mind.

When Lily opened her eyes, Sister Miriam was by her side. Her hands clasped neatly in front of her. Her veiled face turned toward her. Patiently waiting.

'Travel to your heart from your mind. There lies peace, love. There you will find answers to anything you need to know. Wisdom. Clarity. Divinity. It all comes from that place.

'Tend to your soul through quiet contemplation. Reading and self-reflection.

'Take care of your soul. It's the constant companion that's always there as you tread your path.'

Lily breathed the words into her heart. Was she dreaming? Taking a long breath, and she turned to Sister Miriam.

'But who exactly are you?'

'Travel to your heart from your mind. There lies peace, love. There you will find answers to anything you need to know. Wisdom. Clarity. Divinity. It all comes from that place.'

33

Window from a small chapel,
La Verna, Arezzo, Italy.

Spirit Guides.

Blessings while you sit in gratitude.

I'm part of the council of guides and angels who come to support and direct people on their path. You may not realise but it was your soul that cried out to me.

'Anyone who calls with sincerity, consciously or unconsciously, will receive an answer from their spirit guide.

'Know that in this human realm, you're never alone. Be open to signs from us and follow them with the free will that you've been gifted.

'Angels will come too to comfort you when in pain. Just call. They'll give you courage to bear it but pain can't be taken away because it's necessary for lessons you're meant to learn from.'

Sister Miriam's soft voice pulled Lily into the warmth of an invisible embrace.

'I came to comfort you as you sat with your thoughts and fears. And I also come to bless you when you sit in gratitude.

'I'm always with you, guiding and protecting, loving and strengthening you.

Reminding you of the wisdom you already know. I'm always by your side, whatever happens in your life.'

Path at La Verna, Arezzo, Italy.

2. YOUR PATH.

You are Guided.

Impossible to see around the bend.

I s there anything you wish to ask me?'

Lily paused to gather her thoughts. Too many questions but one tumbled insistently to the forefront of her mind.

The words were out of her mouth before she had time to think.

'My future, my destination … please tell me what lies ahead?'

Sister Miriam laughed.

'Only you can walk your path and find out.

'Imagine a winding path and the further you go, the more bends there are. It's impossible to see around the bends.

'But don't fear the unknown. Fear robs us of hope and security and only darkens our way. Set off on your path with gratitude knowing that you're guided and loved.'

Lily felt a rush of happiness as a faint voice deep inside her echoed Sister Miriam's words.

Set off on your path…you're guided… loved.

La Verna Sanctuary view, Italy.

'Everyone's born for a certain purpose. Our first step on our path is to find out what that is in this incarnation.

'Sometimes it can be revealed in meditation. Once you find out, follow that course with free will. Trust, have faith in your destiny. Both the illuminating light of the truthful heart and the illusions of the mind are necessary to navigate this path, achieve harmony and discover your true potential in this life.'

'Sister Miriam, how will I know when I find my path?'

'You will know when you find peace. Have faith, Lily, the way ahead, will become clear.'

'But don't fear the unknown. Fear robs us of hope and security and only darkens our way. Set off on your path with gratitude knowing that you're guided and loved.'

Guided Meditation.

The Garden of Renewal.

L ily stretched her hand out hesitantly toward Sister Miriam's veil.

'I want to see your face.'

Sister Miriam pulled back abruptly.

'Not yet. All in good time.

'Close your eyes and relax. Take a deep breath and breathe deep into your heart as I told you. That's right, in and out.'

Sister Miriam took her hand.

'It's time to take you to a special place, the gardens of La Verna Sanctuary in Tuscany, where I would come to meditate when I lived on Earth, just like you.'

The door flew open and Lily could see a trail of roses along a path.

'Come with me into a special garden, where every colour is an instrument of healing. Each flower has the most exquisite aroma to ease your senses. And each leaf relaxes your body when you touch it.'

Lily found herself outside, floating just above the ground, next to Sister Miriam on a winding path, heading toward a golden staircase.

'Make your way down the steps to the lush grass. Feel how soft and velvety it is, it soothes away your aches.'

Lily smelt the sweet smell of freshly mown grass and sunk her feet into the springy turf.

'Walk with me towards that majestic oak tree. Let's sit underneath and let its leaves give us welcome shade from the warm sun.'

Lily leant her back against the supportive strong trunk, nestling into a dip in its bark. Tension and stress ebbed from her body.

The leaves above swirled in the breeze. She closed her eyes and concentrated on the meandering flow of Sister Miriam's voice.

'Let the mighty oak feed you peace and tranquillity, relax every part of your body.

'It's healing vibrations will relax your breathing and slow down your chattering mind.

'There's nothing to hear, even the birds are still, just the sound of the rustling of leaves. There's nothing to do but relax and breathe, gently and deeply. Then when you're ready open your eyes.'

When Lily opened her eyes, to her astonishment she found herself in a meadow of glorious wildflowers, every colour of the rainbow.

'It's the Garden of Renewal,' explained Sister Miriam.

'Each colour heals a part of the body. Enjoy this special time, revel in the beauty around you. Drink in the strong vibrant colours, the beautiful soft pastels.

'Touch the flowers, admire their beauty. Take in their glorious fragrance and inhale their scent deeply. Feel your cells renewing themselves from their incredible gift.'

Lily felt her body infused with the sweetest of perfumes. She took some deep breaths.

'Go to whichever colour you're drawn to and pick the flower. Lay it on any part of your body that hurts. Sit back and enjoy the colour absorbed into your body.'

Lily bent and plucked a tall golden-headed flower, its petals cascaded over clumps of purple pansies. She held it against her breast and immediately her heart filled with a warm golden light, rushing through her body until it reached the crown of her head, making it tingle.

She felt a surge of joy. Her body felt light. Her feet wanted to move and dance. For a fraction of a second, she saw a girl with golden hair, no more than three or four, twirling in front of her, her arms reaching toward her, round and round she went, faster and faster, the air filled with high-pitched giggles that sent golden waves of love straight into Lily's heart.

Sister Miriam took Lily's hand.

The next minute they were flying through the air.

'Look.'

Below them were, golden fields nestling in the foothills. They continued to glide across the countryside toward a building in a garden of pine trees by an orchard of tall golden sunflowers.

As they whizzed through the garden, Lily felt peace descend. A group of nuns, dressed in the same white tunic as Sister Miriam, were singing in a corner.

'They look like you!'

With a sudden jolt, Lily found herself standing in the garden.

'I was one of these nuns during an incarnation on Earth. This is a St Franciscan Monastery at Mount La Verna.'

Lily's green eyes opened wide.

'How many lives have you had?'

'Many. In this one, I lived in the Order of Poor Clares near the chapel where we met.'

'What are Poor Clares?'

'A women's Order of the Roman Catholic Church. They were devoted to prayer, contemplation and manual work. We observed extreme poverty by fasting and going barefoot. Separate from the world, we embraced solitude and silence, devoting ourselves to worship.'

Lily turned her head and saw a simple hut with brick pillars. Above the central arch was a rose window. A chapel stood to the side with a simple wooden cross on top.

Sunflowers in Arezzo, Tuscany, Italy.

'We lived entirely from alms given by local people.

This principle taught us to live in the moment and with humility.'

'Why's it important to live with humility?'

'Because it's the first step on our spiritual journey. It begins with moving your life from what you want from the world to what the world wants from you. To serve, rather than being served. A time when you cease to exist in a material world and join with the love of the Infinite Creator. St Francis's life of humility was an example we followed. It was a beautiful life of love and peace.'

'There's nothing to hear, even the birds are still, just the sound of the rustling of leaves. There's nothing to do but relax and breathe, gently and deeply. Then when you're ready open your eyes.'

Rocca Maggiore, Assisi, Italy.

The Secret of Life.

Only one way to live.

H ow can I find that peace?' Lily asked.

'It's a magical secret that will protect itself until the person it's shared with has the wisdom and capacity to understand. It comes in two parts.

'The first part is that in the deep part of your soul, you know there's only one way to live. Only one way to act. Only one way to think. Only one way to speak. There are no complicated lessons, no difficult words. The only way is to act, speak and think with love. When this is done all problems fall away.

'When the mind and the ego have their way then you get into difficulties. Stay with love. However hard it is, it's the only way. That way lies truth and peace.'

&

'The only way is to act, speak and think with love. When this is done all problems fall away.'

&

Higher Consciousness.

Listen to the whispers within and ignore the noise.

The second part, Lily, is that higher consciousness can never be known by the mind.

'If you require knowledge, be quiet and go within. If you require solitude, withdraw slightly.

'Be aware of your needs. Be kind and thoughtful not only of others but of yourself. Listen to your quiet voice if it asks you to take time to heal.

'Listen to the whispers and ignore the noise. Listen to your heart and not your mind. This will take courage too as earthly beings love to be doing, and resting has been seen as laziness, instead of the gift it truly is.

'You may look north, south, east, and west and you'll never find what you seek. So, look within and stay in peace.'

Deep in Lily's heart, she heard an echo, louder this time.

'Bring your awareness to your heart and breathe.

I'm a divine soul in a human body,
I'm a divine soul in a human body,
I'm a divine soul in a human body...'

Lily listened to the whispers within.

'There's one undivided consciousness that connects us with our infinite Creator. This energy permeates all living beings on Earth. It's only our ego that creates the false perception of separateness.

'The spark of light within our soul knows no bounds, embraces all beings, love in all its glorious forms. It is Oneness. Where you and I are connected Lily, in space and time. This is your true origin - you are part of the infinite Creator.

&

'You may look north, south, east, and west and you'll never find what you seek. So, look within and stay in peace.'

&

Lake Inle, Myanmar.

3. LIFE ON EARTH.

Reincarnation.

Floating down a river with no compass.

Lily let Sister Miriam's words sink in.
'The spark of light... Connected in love... Oneness. Part of the infinite Creator.'

'There's been such a great shift in consciousness that it can leave people in a state of confusion and upset. Sometimes you may feel that you're floating down a river with no compass.

'The conditions taking place now were always meant to be. I'm with you on your path whether it's smooth or bumpy. With you whether you walk or climb but especially when you falter. With you when you're stopped in your tracks by one of your challenges, with you closer than ever.

'Know that I'm always with you, a gift you've been endowed with for your time on Earth. You've earned it from many lifetimes.

'You volunteered to incarnate at this great time of change and enlightenment. So, walk with me, in peace and light.'

Lily stood up, shocked.

'I've lived on Earth before?'

'Many times. The journey of the soul is endless through many incarnations and many realms. Each one of us on Earth is at a certain stage on our path.

We choose our life path and experiences to learn when we incarnate. It doesn't seem like it when we struggle.

Yet it is that way so that we're able to express our free will to make choices, succeed or fail and in that way, we learn in this earthly manifestation.

'When we sit in meditation, we're able to access the essence of our wisdom and knowledge of our past lives. The past leads us to the present and our actions shape our future.'

'What did you learn from your life on Earth as a nun?'

Miriam looked over at the nuns.

'I always knew an Earthly life was not for me. I needed peace and quiet and was happy to spend hours in silent prayer each day. When I look at the busy lives people lead today, I feel blessed I was able to experience such calm.

'I felt safe within the convent walls and took great pleasure tending the vegetables and flowers that we grew.

'My white habit enveloped me in a cloud of peace. My fellow nuns were of the same mind and only rarely did negative personality traits reveal themselves, leading to interesting conversations among us as well as personal contemplation on mastering the attachments of the ego.

'When I withdrew from the busyness of the world I dwelt in the vastness of silence. Many people would find that a scary place but for me it was where I found heaven. All my answers came from that place. There, I was held in love and faith.

'At certain times we looked after children and I loved seeing their sad faces change with happiness as they began to trust us.

'I passed over after a short illness and was greeted by an immense light, the strength and power for which there are no words. It was all-encompassing and so comforting. I was taken to a place of rest where peace permeated every part of me, around me and through me. I experienced such profound stillness and peace.

'My work with children continued. I tended to children that had passed over. Even though their souls knew where they were, sometimes they acted as if they were still living on the Earth plane and were unsure and confused.'

Lily's heart leapt into her mouth. Her baby…would someone have been there to care for her too? To soothe her confusion and frightened cries?

As if Sister Miriam had read her mind, she continued. *'We never leave them on their own. We escort them to a special place to heal and get used to their new situation. We guide them, hold them and give them whatever they need to adjust and soon they're ready to grow and explore.'*

Out of the corner of her eye, Lily saw a swaddled baby on Sister Miriam's lap. Just as suddenly as it appeared, the vision faded and Sister Miriam was bending over an empty space where the child had been. For a moment there was the sound of a baby giggling…

'It's wonderful to see them gain confidence and become playful again. They're allowed to visit their loved ones on Earth if they wish and are always accompanied and guided.'

Lily had often dreamed about Ruby growing up as a child, her deep green eyes and golden hair. In her dreams she had embraced her…not wanting to let go. Perhaps Ruby had actually visited her, an earthly visit that Sister Miriam was talking about.

'Their souls know all is well and they begin to understand the part they played in their family's lives, even if it was for a short Earth life. They know their paths will meet again and they remain close to their beloved ones for as long as they wish.

'Many things become clearer to them as they learn and develop in the spirit world. It is a joy to be part of this process with them.'

'The conditions taking place now were always meant to be. I'm with you on your path whether it's smooth or bumpy, substitute.'

Lake of Peace Meditation.

Breathe in the power of love.

Take my hand we've more travelling to do. To another special place…'

Lily felt a rush of wind and found herself standing with Sister Miriam on the banks of a lake in a grass meadow covered in exotic flowers overlooked by towering mountains. Lily looked around in awe.

'This is Inle Lake, in Myanmar. This place has its own divine energy and life force. Light and uplifting, open up and connect to it.

'A special lady called Joan loves to visit and teach at these "thin places" where a human's soul on Earth is closer to the souls in the spirit world.'

'Joan?'

'Joan Fountain. She lived on the earth plane as a healer, medium and spiritual teacher for 75 years, passing over at the age of 97 in 2021. She still teaches in the spirit world and returns to Earth from time to time to teach and meditate here.'

A petite old lady, with white hair, wearing a white cloak, with a sweet smile on her face, materialised out of nowhere and sat down cross-legged on the ground.

Lake Inle, Shan State, Myanmar.

Around her, in the haze of the morning mist dozens of young children appeared. Facing them were young men and women who appear to be the parents of these children.

Joan addressed them but it was almost as if she was talking directly to Lily.

'Mothers whose pregnancies don't end with the birth of a living baby or who lose children should know that their little ones do not suffer. Spirit is with them before they pass, bearing them away to places where there's peace and love to heal. They're loved and greatly cared for and grow to adulthood. Send them love for they live on.'

As the mist lifted, Lily caught a glimpse of a child with golden hair with the children. She felt a tight iron band of grief around her heart snap and pure clear air flooded her lungs. Ruby!

Sister Miriam nudged Lily to move nearer to Joan.

'Join me in this meditation,' said Joan.

'You're sitting on the banks of the Lake of Peace. Be still. Be quiet. Listen. All is tranquil. Feel the soft breeze blowing against your cheek. Feel its gentleness. You wait.

'From the waters of the lake, comes the vibration of deep, ever-lasting love. Let the tranquillity of that vibration make you feel at peace. Then a stronger breeze. Feel it blowing through your mind, where the cobwebs of negative conditions of things from long ago are kept.

The wind blows and clears. Sweeps the mind of all the cobwebs of negativity. Blowing them away.

'Your mind's clear and ready now to accept the great love. The soft breeze once again blows gently upon your cheeks. Be still. Be quiet. The vibration of love from the Lake of Peace moves around your body, from top to bottom, and from your waist a spiral of light circles upwards. Twirling around. Be still. Be quiet. Feel the vibration it brings you.

'The light's warm and glows, filling every part of you. Your very soul draws it into itself and is refreshed, making you strong. As the light spirals around you, every cell of your body is refreshed. Healing's taking place and your soul is sending out the joy and love it feels. You are taken to a higher place where the sun shines, sending out spiralling golden rays.

'Be still. Be quiet. Let the tranquillity of love enter your being. As you reach the golden beams there's a golden cup filled with light and love, spilling over the brim. Silvers and golds, amethysts and emeralds, diamonds and sapphires, dazzling colours weaving up and down the spiral, round and around. You've been given the power of love. Bask in the glow of the overflowing cup of love.

'Breathe it in. Breathe it in, my love. Breathe in the power of love, which will help you face all challenges that come to you in life. Be still as the spiral wraps around your body, higher and higher, to the dome of your head with its violet and silver rays of light.

'Bend your head, beloved child, fill up with love. Bend to the higher self and give thanks for the meditation this day. Hold it in your heart and remember it when you need strength and love.

'Be still, my love, be quiet. May the glory that you feel today be with you now and forever more. You're in the Divine Light. Be at rest.'

Sister Miriam whispered in Lily's ear. 'Joan also practices astral travel, perhaps there will be a surprise trip in store for us today. Keep breathing into your soul through the window in your heart. As you breathe out lift your soul a little higher with each breath. You'll feel your soul rising, lifting away from your body. As you rise, you'll see yourself from above sitting in stillness. Don't be afraid. Let go.'

Joan grasped Lily in one hand and Sister Miriam in the other. Lily felt as though she was being swept away like a feather floating on a gentle wind…

Passing over Lake Inle and on….

'From the waters of the lake, comes the vibration of deep, ever-lasting love. Let the tranquillity of that vibration make you feel at peace.'

Awaken to see more than
the eyes can see.

Sunset at Table Mountain, Cape Town, South Africa.

Ecstasy.

Dance in the light, feel its power.

Lily looked around in surprise. She was standing on a flat mountain on a rocky peninsula overlooking a vast ocean. The orange glow of the setting sun reflected in the sparkling water.

Joan turned to Lily and Sister Miriam and smiled. 'We're on the top of the sacred Table Mountain, in the place where two oceans meet. The energy here is strong yet peaceful. I'll leave you here to enjoy the moment, uplift yourselves and give prayers for mankind.'

Then she disappeared like a wisp of cloud.

Sister Miriam moved to the edge. The wide expanse of water stretched for as far as the eye could see. Her face was still hidden beneath the veil. There was a slight sadness in her voice like she was digging deep to find strength to speak.

'Shine and share your light through prayer, kindness, generosity, or peaceful thoughts. Go inwards and find your oasis of peace. Once you're safely there and breathing slowly, send love and compassion to all. Brighten your light and see it surround them.

'Imagine you're a lighthouse, sending out light that will be seen and felt far away. Feel its power transcend the darkness. Your light dispels the darkness. Feel the love pouring out around the world. Dance in this light. Feel its power. Know that only love will end sorrow.'

Totteridge, North London.

Joan's Sanctuary.

Energy Healing.

T ell me more about Joan.'

Lily sat down and waited for Sister Miriam to begin.

'She lived a life dedicated to the work of Spirit. She co-founded The Sylvan Healing Sanctuary in North London in the 1950s with healers Edith Sampson, Bill Brown and Margaret Scandrett.

'They gave energy healing to people who came to the Sanctuary.

Joan was also a medium and a spiritual teacher and she used her gifts to help anyone who came to her seeking help.

In her later years - in her nineties - when she was unable to attend the Sanctuary, she relayed her psychic and prophetic messages through social media and has left a rich legacy of her teachings.'

Hampstead Heath, North London.

4. YOUR SENSES.

Equality.

All are equal and all are love.

I t took a few moments to get her bearings, but when she did Lily found herself alone in a meadow next to a pond. A lone heron stood on one leg at the edge of the rushes, still and elegant, patiently waiting for a ripple in the surface of the water to expose a passing fish. A skein of Egyptian geese flew overhead, long pink legs trailing in the air, white and green wings spread.

Curious, Lily looked around for her travelling guide, Sister Miriam, who was nowhere to be seen. A nearby sign read 'Hampstead Heath, London'.

She took a deep breath. Now was as good a time as any to do a spot of meditation practice, and drop into that peaceful place inside herself.

She took a deep breath in, letting it out slowly.

Her mind clutched at the sight of Ruby sat with the children. How she longed to embrace her.

Her thoughts snatched her out from her peaceful place, shattering the serenity of her mind. Sister Miriam's clear voice cut through the air.

Little Venice, London.

'Look inwards where the fountain of wisdom lies and peace will be found. It is in this place, questions and answers lie alongside each other in simple truths.

'Embark on the journey to higher consciousness where thoughts are pure and wisdom everywhere. Where there are no thoughts of judgement or sorrow, where all is equal and all are love.

'Moments of solitude will help you with this task. Be gentle with yourself when you stumble. It is in falling that you learn humility and it is in rising that you find your strength.'

೮

'Embark on the journey to higher consciousness where thoughts are pure and wisdom everywhere. Where there are no thoughts of judgement or sorrow, where all is equal and all are love.'

೮

Sintra, Portugal.

Awareness.

Respond don't react.

Frustrated, Lily battled to disengage from her nagging thoughts. They pulled at her like sticky tar, refusing to let her go.

She opened her eyes to see Sister Miriam next to her. Her hands neatly folded in her lap.

'It's not unusual to struggle to let our thoughts settle. Our minds are constantly bombarded by thoughts about the past, present and future. Many at the same time, reacting to events and drawing us away from what's happening in the present moment.

'Don't engage with them, don't respond to them, don't indulge them. Be kind to your mind and let them drift away like clouds in the sky.'

Lily's eyes followed the vapour trail of a cloud before it disappeared.

'As you reduce your engagement, focus on your breath for longer periods of time and something remarkable will happen. You'll discover your gift of awareness. With a renewed power to focus you'll become aware of the present moment. At that moment there will be no pre-conditioned reactions. You'll be awakening.'

'Free to choose how to respond, to not react blindly in situations,' mused Lily.

'Exactly. You'll become more aware of not reacting, of accepting others where they stand, of letting go and letting be. Thoughts are habitual. They're not the truth.

'You'll become more aware of how much power you've invested in your thoughts.

'Have you made them the truth? Immovable and inflexible?

Unforgivable, unforgettable?

'Don't hold on to old wounds. Look for the lessons. Look for how experiences have changed you. Look how they set you on a certain path. Look how they gave you choices whether conscious or unconscious.'

Lily felt a distant tug of pain at the remembrance of her child.

'In time you'll even be able to bless your wounds. And then you'll truly experience a miracle of self-love, forgiveness and enlightenment. Knowing you're flawed, yet still loving.'

'You'll become more aware of not reacting, of accepting others where they stand, of letting go and letting be. Thoughts are habitual. They're not the truth.'

Mind Meditation.

It's all perception.

A tidal wave of knowledge washed over Lily, like a download embedding into the very depths of her being. Wisdom that she'd known from the day she was born and had been dormant in her body, waiting to be woken up, recall her past, remembering.

'So, this is how life works,' she thought.

'I experience the world through my five senses - touch, taste, smell, sound and sight as well as mind cognition. The process of perception begins with my consciousness. My mind receives electronic signals through my senses that I translate into sights, sounds and images, that I call reality.

'I register reality depending upon the state and conditioning of my mind. I experience my own version of reality within myself. It's all perception, an illusion.'

The download resonated in her heart like a flame of truth.

She smelt a familiar scent of roses and heard Sister Miriam laugh and clap her hands in childish delight.

'That's right, it's all down to perception. You're becoming aware. When you connect you can appreciate all things, Lily.'

Lily placed her hands against her heart, feeling its reassuring steady solid beat.

'To become more aware of not reacting, train your mind.

When you perceive something happening in your body, you'll feel a sensation. For example, if you see or hear something that makes you angry your body will tense, your heart beat faster, body perspire. Your mind will recognise these bodily sensations as anger and react in flight or fight. This reaction results in us losing control of the situation. This process of reaction is happening all the time as we perceive the world outside us and for that reason, we're not observing and acting in the moment of now.'

Lily scanned her body from her toes to her head, noticing the feelings. An annoying itch on her left elbow. Tingling in her hands. A flutter of excitement in her chest.

'Observe the sensations in your body. Some may feel uncomfortable, some neutral, others pleasant. Observe them with equanimity and detachment. As you get better at this, scan your body up and down in unison with your in and out breath. You are now teaching your mind not to favour any sensations so that you will cease to react in a preconditioned way to what you feel.

'For example, when you're angry your body will not manifest the symptoms of anger and you'll remain calm. You'll learn to act with equanimity in situations and remain mindful at all times.'

Sister Miriam paused.

'Search for that light of truth. It's all around you. Look for love. You'll find it in unexpected places.'

৵

'Search for that light of truth. It's all around you. Look for love. You'll find it in unexpected places.'

৵

The Great Pyramids of Giza, Cairo, Egypt.

5. FORM.

Heart.

Light a candle in your heart.

Sister Miriam slipped an arm around Lily's waist and the next minute they were flying through the air. A cold wind rushed past and a loud roaring filled her ears.

They flew quickly through a narrow passageway underground, emerging into a small chamber lined with thick red granite blocks on bare austere walls.

Goosebumps ran along her arms as she took in the bubbling energy rippling through the air. 'Where are we?'

Sister Miriam sat primly on the floor, pulling her habit tightly around her legs in the darkened room.

'This, my dear, is one of the biggest energy centres on Earth. The King's Chamber in the Great Pyramid in Giza, where King Khufu was buried and it once housed the pharaoh's mummy.'

She patted a place on the floor next to her for Lily to sit down.

'This is the heart of the pyramids, where we'll meditate and absorb this wonderful energy.

'Please, sit comfortably and feel your feet rooted into the earth. Feel the nourishment from the ground travelling up through your feet and into your legs.

'Imagine this beautiful energy taking on a colour, whichever comes to mind, and allow this colour to travel slowly around your body.

'If it wishes to stop somewhere, allow it, and know that it's working to heal that place in your body. The colour may change. Allow its energy to fill your whole body and into your head.'

Lily imagined a blue light sliding across her heart into her chest. The colour of calm, peace and self-awareness. It seemed to be pushing out the grief she'd held in her heart for so long. The coloured light was balancing and healing her. It spread quickly along her arms and legs and back through her feet into the ground, making her feel anchored and strong. She felt a shudder run through her body and let out a sigh of relief. A stray tear rolled down her cheek and fell onto the ground where it instantly evaporated.

'Your heart centre's glowing and pulsing with light. Feel the strength and majesty of this amazing organ. Offer gratitude for the silent and unacknowledged work that it does. So constant and loyal.

'See your lungs expanding and contracting, allowing fresh oxygen and nutrients to be pumped around your body. Imagine the trillions of cells moving, changing and renewing.

'Now give thanks for every organ that quietly and efficiently does its work whether you're aware or not. Feel the love that created your body, the miracle of it, the unparalleled beauty and wisdom it contains.

'Even in the depths of sleep, it renews and grows, heals, and replenishes, silently and freely.

'Like this King's Chamber that's at the heart of the Great Pyramid of Giza and is one of the primary centres of energy on Earth, your heart's your centre of energy, Lily.'

Lily felt overwhelmed with gratitude for her heart that had held her in her grief, kept beating through times she'd felt too exhausted to carry on.

'The human body contains only one centre of consciousness which is the mind. The Sufis, a mystical branch of Islam, through their spiritual experiences, discovered additional inner sense centres - higher consciousness, spirit, intuition and perception.

'In Sufi meditation, they close their minds and open their hearts by breathing into the heart to absorb the energy created by subtle centres in stillness and meditation. The practice creates a feeling of intense ecstasy in the heart as they experience a oneness free from the ties of time, space and form.'

Lily closed her eyes and felt her heart centre glowing like the sun.

Sunset at St Giustino Valdarno, Italy.

'Light a candle in your heart. Take a few moments to breathe slowly and focus on the flame. Notice the different colours in the flickering flame, the intensity of its light. As you look at the flame, feel its warmth wrap around you. Become one with the flame, become light.'

And with that Lily and Sister Miriam were engulfed in a bubble of light and swept from the chamber.

കോ

'Your heart centres glowing and pulsing with light. Feel the strength and majesty of this amazing organ. Offer gratitude for the silent and unacknowledged work that it does. So constant and loyal.'

കോ

Zhinvali Reservoir, Georgia.

Body.

Guardians of our soul.

S trange,' Lily thought as she flew through the air over Zhinvali Reservoir in Georgia and on. 'I feel so much lighter.'

The wisdom Sister Miriam was teaching her must be working its miraculous magic. Her body felt so different from the heaviness of grief she'd felt since the loss of her baby. When each step took effort, like dragging each foot out of mud. How grateful she was to her body for not letting her sink when she had no idea which direction she was headed, when the world no longer had made sense. It had an intelligence all of its own. An innate knowing of what she needed, sending her signs all the time to keep her moving and in balance.

Sister Miriam's reassuring voice cut across her thoughts. Gentle but authoritative.

'Focus, Lily. Focus. Don't distract yourself. Concentrate.'

Sister Miriam had an unerring way of knowing exactly what she was thinking!

'Focus on your breath. Slow it down. Notice your lungs filling and emptying without effort on your part. You don't have to tell them to breathe. Now rest your attention on your heart, beating gently and smoothly in your chest. Observe how it has its own rhythm and wisdom. You don't have to tell it to beat.

81

Isn't your body the most wonderful of miracles? What intelligence created such a machine? You're the recipient of this miracle and its guardian.'

Lily looked down in wonder. She couldn't remember a time when she'd shown appreciation for the frame that carried her. It was her oldest friend – thanks were well overdue. A miracle indeed.

She rested her hands on her legs, still strong and supple. Encircled her fingers around her tiny wrists. Traced scars on her hands, from falling out of trees as a kid, noticed the age spots gracing their backs. Hands that as a child slipped easily into her dad's broad safe ones and as an adult had explored the earth, dived into water, embraced lovers, cradled her newborn child to her breast, and wiped tears of sadness and laughter from her eyes.

Silently she thanked each line on her face, the ones that strode up at the edge of her eyes when she smiled and even the ones that dipped down at the corners of her mouth from past hurts. She'd earned them all. The dips and the troughs. A warm buzzing energy rose up through her chest and up into her throat, pushing up into the crown of her head then swooping back down through her body, her legs to anchor her into the earth.

Her body had carried her this far. She could trust it to carry her further too. The road ahead was unknown but for the first time in a long time, she felt excited, looking toward a future she had once not thought existed. Her face finally turned away from the prison of her past.

'Don't take your body for granted. Do your best for it each day. Thank it for the work it does.

Make peace with it as it ages. Bless this miracle of life. And be grateful for all that it does.'

Lily imagined giving her body a hug. Breathing love into her heart, she sent it out to the tip of her toes and up to the top of her head. Her body sang with energy, she was so thankful to it for the work that it did, the hundreds of miles it had carried her in her life. The uncomplaining feet that had taken her weight…

'Express your deepest gratitude for the privilege of experiencing this earthly life as a human being.'

An outpouring of love and compassion poured into Lily's heart. She felt grateful for the baby she was able to hold in her arms, however briefly. She realised her greatest gift lay in her biggest heartache. Her purpose would be to discover it…

Sister Miriam nodded from behind her veil.

'Embrace this sensation, Lily. Let it fill you up.'

'Whenever you find yourself looking over your shoulder to the sadness of the past and the losses in your life, say these affirmations.

'I accept with humility whatever comes my way. I surrender to each and every experience without fear. With acceptance comes action and with action comes outcome.'

Lily closed her eyes tightly and as she birthed each word into the empty space, another iron band around her heart broke and she was able to take a deeper breath.

Sunset Tuscany, Italy.

Energy.

Raise your vibration and trust.

Raise your vibration. Shine your glory for it is the glory of all that is. Lift your vibration into that of trust. When you do this, layers of fear and uncertainty melt away and you soar up into the higher vibrations of love and peace.'

'How do I raise my vibration? asked Lily.

'In meditation, we can move our breath awareness to our body to observe these vibrations as heat, sensations or colours.

'This field of energy can be cultivated and refined in meditation and is life-changing for the meditator as well as having a positive impact on those that are in contact with this energy field and beyond.'

Lily focused her mind on her breath, moving her sense of awareness throughout her body. She began to feel the vibrations as sparks of light as they moved through her body. She felt connected with everything, with Ruby, as one…

Isle of Bute, Scotland.

Aura.

A special gift.

L ily, we are now at one of the 'thin places' in the Scottish Isles where there is silence and where we're close to the spiritual world, the divine energy of nature, of colours and vibrations.'

Energy bubbled around Lily's body.

She looked at Sister Miriam and saw a glowing light encircling her head like a halo.

'My aura,' said Sister Miriam, as if she'd read her mind. 'You're seeing my energy in colour.

'Around each one of us, there's a circle of light. It's the manifestation of energy that you resonate. With meditation and positive thought, you increase your field of resonance which is uplifting and healing not only for you but those around you.

'Become attuned to it. The power in it is endless. Beyond anything you can imagine.

'It contains all colours of healing and peace for renewal of the soul. It shines outwards to those in need.

'Each aura's unique, like the body form. Your aura's your special gift.

'As with all gifts, it is to be used and given. Held and shared. Acknowledged and given gratitude.'

'What's the colour of my aura,' asked Lily.

And it came to her in a flash…Green like a young shoot and a dazzling emerald. The colour of rebirth, that was the other meaning of her name…Lily. A colour forged in the earth over billions of years of rebirth and renewal.

Rebirth…Renewal…

A warmth flooded her body. The seed of her rebirth had been planted in warm damp earth. Breaking open, its root was emerging, a fragile shoot reaching upwards, its leaves unfurling around the stem. Pushing up through the darkness with an innate knowing as it headed towards the light.

&

'Around each one of us, there's a circle of light. It's the manifestation of energy that you resonate. With meditation and positive thought, you increase your field of resonance which is uplifting and healing not only for you but those around you.'

&

6. RISE AND SHINE.

Blossom.

Nurture your body and mind.

B ut before she could ask, Sister Miriam let out a low chuckle and answered her in the miraculous way she had of reading her mind before she'd said anything.

'All in good time my dear Lily, all will be revealed. But in the meantime, I can see you have many questions to ask me about life, humanity, and the world.

'First, let me take you to your garden at home in London to enjoy the joys of spring together. Come,' said Sister Miriam.

Next second Lily found herself in her garden sat under her cherished blossom tree in full bloom. A place she'd sat each spring on her own, missing Ruby, drawing comfort from the sounds and colours of spring and the future hopes of summer. This time she felt comforted by the presence of Sister Miriam by her side.

'How many minutes of the day do you spend in nature? In its beauty? Stillness and quiet?

'Is it any wonder your body's out of sorts and crying out for peace if you're not replenishing it in nature?

Totteridge, London, England.

'*Seek out more time outside in it each day. Establish a walking routine where you focus on your breath as you look at the flowers.*

'*When was the last time you heard a bird sing? Notice blossom on the tree? Feel the warm glow of sun on your skin?*

'*Many things that don't cost money are overlooked. Small things bring pleasure.*

'*Every day look for joy. You'll find it in places that are closer than you thought.*

'*Nurture your body and mind. Wake up and slowly stretch your body before jumping out of bed.*

'*Create space throughout the day to go within and give gratitude. Turn off the radio or TV so that you're not mindlessly distracted. Take time for a cup of tea without looking at your phone.*

'*Spend time in stillness, stop rushing. Eat for nourishment, not from boredom. Savour each mouthful and bless it quietly.*

'Hone a practice of breath meditation, focusing on your in and out breath to clear your mind. Free it from reactions to past resentments and fears of the future.

'Gradually your mind will move out of a reactive state and into the present moment. You'll become more mindful. Your perception of time will slow down and your clarity of mind will become sharper as you awaken to beauty in all things.'

&

'Is it any wonder your body's out of sorts and crying out for peace if you're not replenishing it in nature?'

&

Sparkle.

Surround the earth with a circle of sparkling light.

Sister Miriam reached out and touched the downward lines at the corners of Lily's mouth.

'There will always be suffering in this world. People, animals, the planet. Life's suffering.'

'Why?'

'Because all existence on earth is based on the principle of opposites. Good and bad, compassion and cruelty, love and hate, peace and war, humility and pride and so on. Each difficult experience is a learning to open us up to become more patient and tolerant. To truly appreciate joy, one needs to also experience sadness. To enjoy the fragrance of a rose, one needs to experience the prick of the thorn.

'People need to find their path, exercise free will, individually and collectively, to negotiate through the breakdown they may experience on Earth.

'Rapid changes in the form of wars and destruction through natural disasters caused by climate change are occurring. Light is needed to ensure these changes are positive.

'So, shine as brightly as you can. Light your inner candle and light another's.

'Spread joy with a circle of sparkling light. Glowing bright and strong.

Basilica of Saint Francis of Assisi, Italy.

'Your joy's needed now. More than ever, to help people who suffer or remain in darkness.

'As long as you have faith, spirit guides like me can come and help guide you.

'As you know, you can also draw strength by meditating. Breathing into your heart - patience, tolerance and courage.

These will help you navigate through challenges and when you pass through them, you'll be stronger for it. With this strength, you can help others.'

'So, shine as brightly as you can. Light your inner candle and light another's.

'Spread joy with a circle of sparkling light. Glowing bright and strong.'

La Verna Sanctuary, Meditation Cave of St Francis of Assisi,
Arezzo, Italy.

Compassion.

Everything happens for a reason.

Much upheaval's happening to people and the planet right now and it's hard to distance yourself from all this suffering. But know that nothing happens that's not meant to.

'When distress upsets and brings you down, centre yourself to share love.

'Take time to send out love and light to whoever and wherever you feel it's needed It is your intention that comes from your heart that matters. Your prayers and good deeds, kindness and smiles to strangers, are the love that will help heal the world.'

Sister Miriam paused to let her words sink in.

'But remember...'

Lily looked up.

'...act with the utmost kindness and compassion.

'Help them with love and wisdom but do not divert them from their learning experiences. Compassion is about acting exclusively in the best interests of another and not about giving relief to your conscience or guilt.'

Lake Como, Italy.

Courage.

The ego loves to fear.

In this world of opposites what's the inverse of fear?' asked Lily.

'Courage.'

'Fear is the most destructive force. It is vital to stand in your light and stand up to the darkness. Shine with love and hope. Stay on the path you know is true. Stay in love.

'Fear weakens and diminishes. Stay true to your wisdom and faith. However hard, keep coming back to it if you falter. The light's always there for you to find.

'Don't give in to fear. That's not your path, your journey. It is not your mission.

'By its very nature fear holds us back from moving forward and experiencing the richness of life and the experiences it can offer.

'Sufi poet Rumi said: "Run from what's comfortable. Forget safety. Live where you fear to live."

'Courage is not the absence of fear but the overcoming of it. With fear, we limit our development. It holds us back from experiencing freedom, love and compassion. Fear is diminished with wisdom and truth and a realisation of our infinite soul.'

Ephesus, Kusadasi, Aegean, Turkey.

7. WISDOM.

Kindness.

A tiny candle lights up a dark room.

Lily my dear, each one of us can alleviate suffering for others by offering the light of kindness.

'How the light of a tiny candle lights up a dark room.
How the light of the stars lights up the night sky.
How one kind deed or thought ripples out into the world.
Beyond anything, we can see.

'When we experience pain and receive kindness from others it opens us up to a new softness of love and compassion.

'One needs to experience kindness. Kindness to oneself and the humility of receiving kindness from others. What you receive you're able to recognise and give out.

'The secret of giving lies with the heart. The place where kindness, compassion and love reside. Live intuitively in this way. One can also be hurt that way but it's a price well worth paying. There's always a price!'

An entrance, La Verna Sanctuary, Arezzo, Italy.

Faith.

Trust in the Unknowing.

We may never understand why people suffer and die,' said Lily vehemently, thinking of her tiny baby snatched from Earth too soon. 'So, we need faith.'

'Exactly. Not knowing but still believing that good will arise. Not giving in to the darkness but being the strength and prayers for those who don't have faith.'

Lily recalled how meditating on her breath had taken her to a state of expanded awareness, where her grief had faded away and she'd felt peace.

'Return to that place when you're impacted by the highs and lows of everyday life,' said Sister Miriam, as if reading her thoughts. 'It enables you to accept events that come your way knowing that there's nothing permanent but change.

'Live in freedom in the moment knowing that with acceptance comes action and with right action a positive change.'

Courtyard, La Verna Sanctuary, Arezzo, Italy.

Light.

Light another's way and light your own.

L ight someone's way, Lily.' Sister Miriam's words echoed in Lily's mind.

She recalled how at her lowest ebb she'd drawn strength from a kind word from a stranger or a smile.

'Lift someone's spirit. Offer a kind word, help. However small, these are some of the many ways in which you can light someone's way.

'And when you light another's way you immediately light your own.

'It spreads and multiplies, and this is how darkness will fade. Slowly but surely with love and kindness, service and devotion.'

When I learn to love myself, I can feel compassion and share it with others, thought Lily.

'How do I begin?' asked Lily earnestly.

'The first step is to work on reducing our defects and putting into practice our virtues; like kindness, patience, charity, generosity, and selflessness. Such acts create a finer energy within oneself that will open us up on this path of love.'

ॐ

Look for the diamond who tells the truth without fear or favour.

Jerusalem.

Truth.

Truth is truth.

Sister Miriam, I feel privileged to receive your help and guidance but I still don't truly understand why. Is there a reason you've come to help me now and not before?'

'It's time to tell you the painful truth.'

Lily tensed.

'As you know, the world's going through a turbulent time. Negative energy created by mankind from its exploitation of this earth and its resources has tilted the ecological balance. In addition, man's inhumanity to man is causing huge hardship. Much like when iron ore goes into the smelter it comes out as steel, man's inability to change his ways voluntarily to improve the world in which we live and how we live means that only catastrophic events will force this change.

I'm here to guide you and others like you with a kind heart to follow the spiritual path. To help others navigate the difficult times that are upon us until the coming of the energies of a new consciousness for mankind.

'Those that hear the truth and are touched by it, will recognise it. Those that are not ready to hear it will walk away. It is not for you to persuade them or be upset by their response.

'Truth is truth. Some will crave it, others will scoff. It is important to stay humble and respectful of others' journeys.'

'As I guide you, your inner self will also speak to you. Together we'll take you on your path of truth and prepare you for the journey ahead.'

'How will I recognise the truth?'

'In the mystic Sufi meditation tradition, a branch of Islam, a person goes into ecstasy when he experiences the truth. This may be when listening to the words of a master, music or in meditation. Such is the power of the energy of truth that it resounds in every cell in our body.'

At these words Lily felt an overpowering energy pervade through every cell, an extreme happiness she hadn't felt since the birth of her daughter. She threw back her head and laughed enjoying the swirl of ecstatic energy and knew in that instant, Sister Miriam had told her a sacred truth.

Bruge, Belgium.

8. ATTACHMENTS.

Vibrations.

Hear the rumble of the earth.

L ily listened hard.

'*Sense the deep changes that are happening. It was never going to be easy. And it was never going to be without huge suffering.*

'*The Earth's vibrations are shifting and if you're quiet, you can feel it. If you're still, you can sense it.*'

Below Lily's feet, from somewhere deep within the earth, she felt a gentle pulse.

'Everything is energy vibrating, including you and me. Increase your levels of vibration through meditation. The higher the vibration the more positive you feel and this is also felt by those around you.

'At a subtle level, one can tap into memories of past lives and gain knowledge of the Universe, where vibrations of all our activities exist. This can provide insights into the future as well. The knowledge available is infinite, and the only limiting factor is our capacity to hold it.

'And you can connect with people like me, the spirit of those who have passed over before. Glean knowledge from these disincarnate beings wanting to transmit guidance for the betterment of humanity.'

❧

Prague, Czech Republic.

Change.

Break free from attachment to desires and old habits.

It's time to change my dear, Lily. Some changes have already happened for some people.

'After the pandemic, many discarded old ways and accepted simpler ways of living. They lowered expectations and found less stressful ways of living.

'Many over the centuries have learned that the simple life is the most beneficial for spiritual learning and practice. You're now firmly on this road.

'Old habits and desires drop away to be changed forever, never to be desired again."

'Tell me about the journey of the soul.'

'The soul personality of an individual is built over many incarnations and change in one lifetime is not easy. It can be like a snail crossing the face of the moon.

'True change takes place when we encounter intense adversity that shakes our very foundations and makes us reflect as we sit and contemplate it in meditation. The pandemic is only the beginning...'

Strasbourg, France.

Letting Go.

Perceived problems.

D id you know so many perceived problems come from the state of your mind. They're not real. Borne from insecurities, judgements, fears and opinions from others as well as yourself. Life can be peaceful, it's in your hands.

'Think of the times when you've experienced peace and calm. Even if it's just for a few moments. It's not because suddenly all your problems have been solved. It's because you've not allowed a barrage of thoughts to have control. For a moment or two, you've entered a state of peace and experienced the state of love. These states are eternal.

'A child's state of mind is naturally joyous but as we grow older, we become more conditioned by our environment and the influences of those around us. Our parents, family, schoolteachers... Our joy gets masked by layer upon layer of conditioning.

'Meditation is the process of erasing that conditioning, much like removing files on a computer so that the hard disc operates efficiently. And the natural joy of the mind begins to shine through.

'The meditator manifests the joyous mind of a child but with grown-up wisdom.'

Island of Hydra, Greece.

9. EMPATHY.

Understand others.

Accept another as they are in that moment.

Lily my dear, we're not born to live in isolation. On Earth, we live in community with family and friends. Learning how to live with others has a profound influence on your state of mind.

'The way you choose to react to words, deeds or another's actions is your choice. You cannot control what others say or do. Your reaction is a huge part of whether you're affected deeply or can transform into a more accepting and loving being.

'It's so easy to react. We have infinite words with which we can prove to the other person that our way is best, that we are right. We can choose to withdraw our love, turn our backs in sour silence. Be cruel or insensitive.

'It's good to remember that these are choices. Nobody can make you react. They can trigger you. Taunt you, play on your insecurities, make you feel less than or even feel superior.

'But know that when you decide to sit with your feelings for a short while instead of reacting, you can be aware of your true self – love and peace. And know that reacting is about ego games.

Lake Como, Italy.

'Sitting in silence will bring you wisdom and awareness. You can sit with someone in anger or sadness in a way that is neither confrontational nor judgmental. Just accepting another as they are in that moment.'

'No reaction and acceptance of another at all costs are powerful disciplines. Buddha said, "To understand everything is to forgive everything," meaning that if we put ourselves in the place of the other, leaving aside our ego, we can have compassion.'

'Sitting in silence will bring you wisdom and awareness. You can sit with someone in anger or sadness in a way that is neither confrontational nor judgmental.'

Voice and Tone.

Catch yourself when you use unkind words.

It's not just what and how you say it to others, but it also matters how you address yourself.

'*Take care in the way you talk and the words you speak. Be kind to yourself, talk in a way you'd address a friend.*

'*At the end of each day reflect on your attitude towards yourself. Were you impatient and brusque? Scathing and unloving? Often this has become a habit and you're not even aware of it.*

'*The cumulative effect of unkind words can affect your mood and how you feel about yourself and life.*

'*Catch yourself when you use critical and unkind words. Be self-reflective and note what needs attention.*

'*Use appropriate language, encouraging and loving. If you're constantly critical of yourself, you're no doubt critical of others without even intending to be.*

'*Listen to the tone of your voice. Does it sound condescending or uplifting? Is it loving or critical? The more self-awareness you have, the easier it will become.*

'*We're creatures of habit and years can go by without anyone pointing these things out. And maybe when they do, it is met with defensiveness and surprise.*

'Often, it's not the truth that hurts but the tone of voice in which it is said. Always speak the truth at the right time, with good intent and compassion to help. Be silent if you wish to tell the truth just to unburden yourself when it's of no benefit to the other person. Then let go of your burdens in meditation.'

ॐ

'Listen to the tone of your voice.
Does it sound condescending
or uplifting?
Is it loving or critical?
The more self-awareness you have,
the easier it will become.'

ॐ

Lake Trasimeno, Umbria, Italy.

Good Deeds.

Instigate small acts of charity.

K indness is so important,' reflected Lily. She recalled how unkind she had been to herself in her grief. Blaming herself for the death of her child. Telling herself she was stupid or silly when things went wrong in her life. She made an intention to talk to herself in a kinder way.

'Small acts of kindness have their own beautiful energy, that spreads and multiplies. See the power and enormity of these acts.

'Never think that any kind gesture's too small. Be aware of the impact your acts have had and the important part you have still to play in evolving consciousness.

'You are here, as everyone is, for a reason and are playing your part without necessarily seeing the result.

'Let your faith guide you and your intuition prod you if you go astray. Let your love be all-encompassing and your words gentle and kind.

'There is cause and effect of every good deed no matter how small – the law of karma. But equally, we must not be attached to the results of our actions and in that way, we experience true freedom.

'In this world of form, there is also collective Karma. If as a civilisation we abuse the earth and humanity, we all suffer the consequences of our collective actions. This is the destiny we create for ourselves.

'In addition to the pragmatic actions we can take to do the right thing, spiritually we can sit in meditation and send the energy of love and healing to humanity and Mother Earth.'

಄

'There is cause and effect of every good deed no matter how small.'

಄

-

Simplicity.

Celebrate the glory of the natural world.

T*he key to life is simplicity.*

'*There's more love than hate, more hope than despair and more good than wickedness in this world.*

'*Remember that. Take those thoughts with you when you enjoy the natural world, by the sea or in the countryside. Part of the true glory of being in nature is not being bombarded by all the negativity humans create.*

'*Don't let grey clouds cast their fear and sorrow over you. Be aware and don't allow this to happen so often.*

'Life on this earth is a gift but what good's a gift if we don't live life to its fullest?

'As I've said before, be present in it, don't live in the past or the future.'

Lily placed her hands over her heart and gazed at the orange and yellow streaks of the setting sun.

Hesitantly, she repeated Sister Miriam's words that had found a haven in her heart.

'Meditation allows me to be present in the moment and experience this glory. By centring my awareness on the tip of my nose, focusing on the in-breath, the out-breath. My awareness is the first step on the ladder of awakening.'

She took a deep breath in…

'You've listened well, Lily. Lose yourself in the beautiful sunset, become it. This moment's yours.'

Lily found herself pulled into the vibrant colours, merging and blending until she was alive with the energy of oranges and yellows, colours sliding through her body, feeding her soul.

'You're awakening, becoming alive. You're opening your eyes to see the beauty in everything.'

'Awareness is the first step on the ladder of awakening.'

10. EXPAND YOUR HEART.

Positivity.

Start each day with positivity.

S o,' mused Lily, slowly coming out of her reverie. 'Events in our lives are neither good nor bad. Just what we make of them. The outcome shaped by our state of mind?'

'Exactly. A positive mindset leads to positive action, resulting in a positive outcome.'

Lily thought for a while. She could transmute the pain of her past by seeing the positive in it... Take the negative out of the memory of the tiny girl she was forced to let go. Release the sadness in her soul of never having the opportunity to be the mother she wanted to be on Earth.

She was determined to see beyond her unhappiness, dig out the self-pity. As she made her intention, a volcano of fire erupted in the pit of her stomach, ejecting a furious energy and snapping more of the iron rings caging her heart.

One...Snap! Two...Snap! Three...Snap! Four...SNAP!

More of the cloying black grief and despair she'd carried for so long, left her body and dissipated in the night air.

Awareness is the first step on the ladder of awakening.

Lake Inle, Shan State, Myanmar.

In the haze of the dipping sun just before darkness claimed the sky, a girl with golden hair like a halo appeared in the silhouette of the dying sun.

And Lily's heart felt a surge of joy and recognition.

The love she had for her child would always keep them connected, an invisible thread that bonded them forever. Her child may not be physically with her, but she would always be a part of her and for that she was grateful.

Sister Miriam's voice cut across her thoughts.

'Both painful and joyful experiences are of use to others. It'll give you joy passing your wisdom and knowledge on to others.

'Know that each candle you light will be used to light another. In this way, you spread the light. Ignite the flames of peace and understanding.'

'Positivity arises from a peaceful mind as does virtue result from positive intent and action. A peaceful mind is created by meditation.

'Let go of negative thoughts and past resentments. Generate positive thoughts and behaviour. We are what we think. Have the courage to overcome fear as it takes us down a road of inaction and negativity.

'Positivity harnesses the immense power of the mind to act courageously.

'When you are aware or mindful, you're in the present moment. Free from negative thoughts and resentments of the past and not anticipating fears of the future.
'The moment of now is one which begins with nothingness so fill it with positivity.

'What you do now will shape your future.'
Lily focused on the joy in her heart and made a vow to herself to look for the best in people and situations.

'Start each day with positivity, with a determined effort to not be dragged down by the illusion of darkness.'

Sister Miriam took Lily's hand.

'Come, we have another journey of the soul to take.'

Lake Inle, Myanmar.

Shine and share.

Elevate yourself to help others.

Sister Miriam and Lily flew over Inle Lake, in Shan State, in Myanmar.

'What a beautiful sight' remarked Sister Miriam as they saw so many novice young monks dressed in saffron robes sat cross-legged in the open monastery.

'They're all sitting in meditation. Even children practice meditation here from an early age. They learn to live in peace within themselves and with each other. The vibrations of joy these children create in this place are so beautiful, you'll feel uplifted and happy.

'You can help others by changing yourself and raising your vibration.'

'Through meditation.'

'Yes. It's a power to help you raise your vibration and lift another's soul by raising their vibration in turn. On a higher frequency, you have the ability to soothe someone's wound, calm someone's anger.

'These are your ways of using your light. Send those beams out to your environment, neighbours, friends. Shine and share. Elevate yourself so you help others.'

'Einstein said, "Everything in life's vibration",' said Lily.

Novice monks at Phaya Taung Monastery, Lake Inle, Myanmar.

'He was right. Everything that looks solid vibrates at a particular level. Every aspect of a human being, physical, mental or spiritual vibrates at differing frequencies.

'The higher the vibration the greater the wellbeing and the energy of the person.

'Vibrations are also the medium through which we communicate intuitively with one another. During meditation, we lift our vibrations. Our higher vibrations can also be sent out to others to uplift them.'

Lily focused hard and sent out a prayer. To wherever the soul of her child was, whichever dimension she was in, to receive a message of love from her earthly mother.

A rising hot fire rose in her belly into her heart, her throat, up into the crown of her head and out into the ether. A surge of green love energy.

Lily's eyes followed the stream of energy shooting through the air. In the shape of a nearby cloud, she could see the face of a girl with a golden head of hair. Ruby! This time she was turned toward her and she could see her dazzling emerald eyes shining straight into hers, smiling. Just for a moment.

Then she was gone, leaving a golden glow in her heart.

ॐ

Step away from the canvas and you
will see the bigger picture.

Temple of Seti 1, El-Balyana, River Nile, Egypt.

Generosity.

Expand your heart.

As more chaos appears in the world it's even more important to stay true to your values. Make things as simple as you can. Share your light and vibrations as wide as you can.

'Put aside earthly matters and try to just see the light around everyone. Know that the light in your hearts is joining with millions of others with love in their hearts. Imagine the power.

'Visualise the light going wherever it's needed most. See it travelling far and wide. Nothing can dispel this light with love at its core.

'Expand your heart. Control your thoughts.
Be generous in all ways, especially with your words.'

ॐ

'Expand your heart.
Control your thoughts.
Be generous in all ways, especially
with your words.'

ॐ

Insight.

The big picture…

Do not despair of the way you see the world. As being always bombarded with negative visions of the world, you can feel weary trying to keep uplifted and positive.

'You cannot change many things. In fact, the very circumstances that are upsetting you are the ones that will provoke the change that is needed.

'Because you are limited to what you can see and what is presented, it is impossible to see the bigger picture. No one sees the million acts of kindness carried out in these situations.

'If you could see people's hearts opening to one another, people sharing food and their time, you would feel full of hope.

'But rarely do you see this. So, you focus on how much misery and suffering there is. And indeed, there is, but many souls are travelling their path and their souls have chosen this growth.

'The human logical mind finds it hard to understand but this is where trust and faith must prevail.'

'The closer you are to the picture the less you will see. As you meditate you become compassionately detached. Detachment from one's biases, prejudices and attachments that plague us in the human form.

In this way giving us the freedom and the objectivity to actively help others with positive compassion.

'You step outside of the smaller picture and can see more.

'You can maintain your peace amid turmoil. Both can co-exist at the same time like two sides of a coin.

'You gain insight to see across time and space the value of learning in every action and deed.'

❧

Sunrise at the Great Pyramid of Giza, Cairo, Egypt.

11. AWAKEN.

Turn Towards the Light.

Find the sacred space inside you.

Dear Lily, as we travelled through the Nile to the pyramids, we saw some amazing monuments. The pyramids are truly a great wonder of the world. These people had wisdom way beyond our understanding.

'The quest of our lives on Earth is to acquire wisdom.

'Find the sacred space inside you where the incessant chatter is quiet and wisdom can be found.

'You'll rediscover a well of prayer inside you. The depths of love and strength to give you hope. Strengthen and hold you. Surround you and protect you from fear.

'You've overcome darkness before and you will again. By turning towards the light, the shadow falls behind you.

'When you hit a crossroads in your life, choose the path of hope not fear.

'Sit in contemplation meditation and focus on your goal. Visualise and play out what you wish to achieve in your mind's eye. The positive power of the mind will guide you to your destination.'

ॐ

Abu Simbel Temples, Aswan, Egypt.

Gratitude.

Gratitude for all things.

Lily, with gratitude, you'll naturally look on the brighter side of life.

'Look at the world in awe, with gratitude for all things.
Big or small, pain or pleasure, ignorance or wisdom,
all these things bring gifts of learning. Accept them
with humility.'

'Look at the world in awe,
with gratitude for all things.'

Acceptance is the first step in the journey of humility.

Island of Hydra, Greece.

Acceptance.

Humbled by nature's beauty.

L ily felt Sister Miriam's hand firmly in hers as she looked down over the Greek islands.

'Lily, how we're humbled by the outstanding beauty of nature that surrounds us. See as we pass over Hydra.

'Smell the fragrance of the trees after the rain. See the beauty of the bulbs pushing from the darkness of the earth towards the sun. Enjoy the colours of nature and know beauty.

'Inhale fresh crisp and invigorating air. Let it fill your lungs with energy.

'Fill your ears with the melody of fauna and let your body sway with its enticing music.

'Count the stars in a night sky and bask in the magnificence of our Universe.

'Walk barefoot along a beach and imagine each grain of sand contributing to the whole. Wonder at the rise and swell of waves in the ocean. Treasure how much beauty there is in this world.'

Autumn in La Verna, Arezzo, Italy.

Know Yourself.

Sit for a moment to quieten.

L ily, know yourself and the purpose of your present life on Earth.

'Sit quietly. Breathe and get to know yourself. Where you are. Where you have come from. Where are you going. What you are doing. What are your thoughts. What you could do better. What small things would make a difference for you and others. Do you spend your time wisely? Do you rest? Move? Are your thoughts mindful or do they race off at tangents all day?

'Aristotle said knowing yourself is the beginning of all wisdom.

'A wise man, indeed. The path begins with a first step of awareness. Not just about the world outside but the journey inside of you through observing your breath in meditation.

'Awareness is the key to the door of self-realisation, of awakening. Slowly, veils are removed revealing your true path in this incarnation, showing you the beauty of the unseen and unknown. Once discovered, you'll never wish to turn back from this beautiful path.'

Every human being is presented with opportunities. We need sight to recognise them and courage to exercise them.

Pienza, Siena, Italy.

Luck.

There are no coincidences, no good or bad luck.

L ily sat at Sister Miriam's feet, listening intently.

'We make our own luck through karma, our good deeds that we do with our own free will.

'There are no coincidences, no good or bad luck.
Our souls chose to be on Earth at this momentous time. We
all knew the importance of the work we were meant to do.

'Any trials and tribulations you've gone through on Earth
were agreed before you incarnated. Each step you took along
your path was for your growth. Whether you made mistakes,
you followed your path even if you didn't walk in a straight
line. In fact, it was the bends in the path where you stumbled
that taught you the most.

'Every soul is here for a purpose and has a path to travel. And yet we sleepwalk through life forgetting the purpose of our existence.

'Living with regrets and resentments until the end when it is too late. Look inside at the power that lies within. Rise up and accept your mission. Elevate yourself. You have wings, fly.'

Olive Grove, Verona, Italy.

12. REBIRTH.

Stay on the Path.

The journey's yours alone.

There are many paths home and yours is not the same as others.

'We can exercise our free will, take responsibility for our actions and never blame others. Be aware of opportunities as they present themselves and have the courage to act upon them.

'Lily my dear, the future is unknown so that you can learn to act wisely and exercise your free will to achieve your goals in life. You also need to have faith, a belief that your outcome will be a positive one. You must experience both failure and success and, in that way, learn humility.

'Ultimately you will learn to accept the outcome of your efforts, whatever they may be.'

You must experience both failure and success and, in that way, learn humility.

Loro Ciuffenna, Tuscany, Italy.

Breathe.

Lift your spirits.

ily, it is important to be aware of how your body reacts. When it's triggered in an uncomfortable situation, it goes on high alert and tightens.

'Now think of the joy it feels when you hear an innocent baby giggle, see a sunset or hear the sounds of a flowing river. Your spirits lift and for that time you breathe that bit deeper and slower. Even if it is only for a moment.'

Lily thought about how her body reacted to adverse situations with feelings of tension. And how the mind reacted to those feelings by recalling similar memories of adverse past experiences. Often, she lost an ability to be rational, act objectively and in a considered manner in those situations as emotions got the better of her.

Terranuova Bracciolini, Tuscany, Italy.

Freedom.

Reborn into new thinking.

Lily, there's nothing permanent in this life on Earth but change. So, awaken and change yourself. Embrace it.

'Burst out of your shell. Be reborn into new thinking and new behaviours. New thought forms where others are no longer a threat, neither inferior nor superior but all are equal. I know you yearn for this new way of thinking. Deep down this has always been a desire in your heart.

'Every human being once they've awoken finds freedom of the mind. Freedom from past resentments and attachments. Travel light. It is time for you to live in the now, sincere and truthful with a clear conscience.'

Park Guell, Barcelona, Spain.

Oneness.

Avoid judgement on another's road.

We're often quick to judge others and put others down to feel superior. Our ego loves to do that. But we're all travelling on the same path, some are ahead of us, some behind, some walking alongside.

'There are many roads to travel, all depending on your soul's needs. Keep your eyes on your road and don't judge another's. This is most important to remember.

'As you walk your path, walk in gratitude for your opportunities to learn, give, teach and to accept.

'As you know Lily, even the opportunity to suffer offers you gifts of wisdom, humility and gratitude. Know what these gifts are and offer gratitude for them. Know your strengths and weaknesses. Accept them all and know they're opportunities for growth.

'We tend to judge people only by their outer garb, quick to judge through our own lens, knowing little about their lives, experiences and evolution. What's there to judge if we accept that all of us are on the same path?

'Meditation helps to connect at an energetic spiritual level of oneness where we find we're all the same separated only through the perception of earthly time and space.'

Galway, Ireland.

13. ELEVATE YOURSELF.

Anchor.

Tides are strong.

Lily, every time you feel unsettled bring your awareness to your breath and you will feel calm and peaceful.

'Tides can be strong and although this is needed to wash away old thoughts and established patterns, they can throw you off balance.

'To keep sure-footed, root yourself in faith. Be strong in intent and resolute in trust. That is what you must focus on when the waters around you are turbulent. You have your anchor. Don't be knocked off course.

'Feel the weight of your anchor keeping you on the path to the light.'

Church of The Holy Sepulchre, Jerusalem.

Higher Self.

When your light's dim, someone will share theirs.

W hat's the higher self, Sister Miriam?'

'The source of direction and wisdom.'

'How do I find it?'

'Through your intuition. A knowing that's at your very essence and part of your higher soul. You do not doubt these feelings or thoughts when they come. In fact, you welcome them and recognise they're part of the wisdom that you were allowed to bring with you into this lifetime.

'Many times, you've acted upon it and sometimes ignored it, only to be nudged and prodded until you do act upon it, even if this comes years later and shows up as a similar situation or with the same person or someone different.

'How wondrous it is when you recognise your higher self at work. There is much to be grateful for this unique blessing.

'It never gives up on you, patiently waiting in the background to nudge again and again until you open your eyes and hearts.

'Think how many ways you've been blessed throughout your life. In good times and bad how you been carried. The help you've received from unexpected quarters. How things have turned out better than you may have hoped.

'If you've had to change your path and step into the unknown, your higher self has quietly been beside you - helping, cajoling, soothing, encouraging and loving.

'Always live in gratitude. Never in fear. You can notice easily those who do and they stumble many times without the solid faith that you have.

'This life is not always easy, sometimes painful, but feel the light of the higher self around you. When your light's dim, your higher self will light a tiny match to see you through the next step.

'In deep meditation, your soul leaves your body as you journey to embrace the greater light. This is where your higher soul resides. And there the conversation of the deepest knowledge takes place.'

ॐ

Ponte Vecchio, Florence, Italy.

Peace.

Hold a vision of tranquillity.

S ister Miriam, will there ever be peace on Earth?'

'*Hold in your mind a vision of peace, calm, a coming together of differences. Forgiveness and a love for all.*

'*Use your imagination to visualise the holding hands, especially between people who are quarrelling. Imagine an outstretched hand of peace. A gentle hand on a shoulder of reassurance and comfort.*

'*Your vision will accompany people's prayers from around the world to add strength to the goal for peace. The simplest acts, can bring peace. Use your daily life to bless another. To give comfort. A word. A smile. A silent hug.*

'True peace is experienced from the inside out.

'Practice this affirmation. I express my deep gratitude for the unique privilege of experiencing this earthly life as a human being and spreading peace.

'As you do this, you'll experience a feeling of inside-out love and compassion. Embrace this sensation as it fills you up and you'll experience true peace.'

Vineyards of Verona, Italy.

In the Moment.

The art of being.

Lily, the most simple acts, can bring you such peace.

'Many people have lost the art of just being. Be with your thoughts in a positive way. Just keep being aware.'

'Use the anchor of your breath, like a switch to turn on the light of awareness. This brings you into the illumination of the present moment, where you can see clearly.

You will know that this is the right moment as you are covered with peacefulness. If you are in nature, you will be absorbed into its sounds, shapes and smells and you will experience its intense beauty.

You are being in peace.'

Spring flowers in Tuscany.

14. REALISATION.

Spring fever.

Turn towards the sun.

Sister Miriam and Lily watched the sun rise, giving birth to the day ahead.

Sister Miriam smiled as Lily closed her eyes to enjoy the first rays of the sun warming her face.

'Every morning we're born again, just like every spring is the birth of another season of hope and joy.

As winter fades and the days become longer and brighter, it is time to turn our faces toward the sun. Feel the gentle warmth that coaxes flowers from their dark resting place and know that you too are being asked to grow. Feel the cloak of darkness slip away and look around for the multitude of spring miracles.

'*Let each delicate bud remind you of your strength.*
Every shade of leaf and flower fill your hearts with joy and remind you of your beauty.

'*Work on your upliftment, turning towards the sun, feeling the vastness of the sky. Let nature fill you with wonder and renewal. Breathe it in as deeply as you can and fill your body with love. See the beauty around you and give thanks.*'

'Buddha said, "when you realise how perfect everything is you will tilt your head and laugh at the sky".

'And so, as you continue with your mediation practice and develop your awareness the veils that have been drawn between you and nature over the years are lifted one by one. One begins to awaken to the potential of the soul and its natural joyfulness and so begins a deeper appreciation and respect for the earth we all come from.

'Just seeing the magnificence of a single flower, from seed to bud, from blossom to decay - tells the story of the impermanence of our lives. Lifetimes hold only so many springs.

'Beauty is in the eye of the beholder, and the veils you lift to see that beauty depend on wisdom you've accessed along the way.'

Sintra, Portugal.

Consciousness.

A new way is coming.

It is time for change as people know and many desire. People are beginning to realise they don't need so much and are turning back to nature to provide.

'From misery, there will come understanding and a wish for deep change and a desire to live in peace with neighbours. After chaos, people will find peace in their hearts and pool their resources.

'Nothing belongs to anyone. All is for everyone. No one will be excluded. The time of greed and selfishness is coming to an end. The chaos and misery it has caused is plain for all to see. People will welcome this new way. This blessed opportunity for giving.

'We'll look back and reflect on extravagances and waste, shake their heads in disbelief. A new way is coming.

'Your task Lily, is to welcome it with outstretched hands. Feel the peace within you as you help to birth it.'

'The pace of change for humans is slow, usually after many incarnations, and often even when we change our ways, we default back to old, unhealthy habits.

'Change comes when we begin to accept impermanence and more importantly experience it.

'Buddha said: "Better a single day of life seeing the reality of arising and passing away, than a hundred years of existence remaining blind to it".

'He was referring to the experience of impermanence.

When you sit in meditation and observe the sensation in your body with equanimity you will experience the ebb and flow of the sub atoms particles that make up much of our body, arising and passing away, like a flow of vibrations. There is no central command.

You will experience that nothing within us is permanent. 'We are all the same -one- energy, divided by our perceived egos that creates an illusion of separation.'

Kazbegi Mountains, Caucasus, Georgia.

15. JOAN'S HEALING.

School of Life.

Questions.

Sister Miriam turned to Lily with a smile.

'Would you like to accompany me today to Joan's spiritual teaching school? She chooses the most beautiful locations. Today it's taking place in a remote monastery in the Caucasus under Mount Kazbek, one of the highest volcanic mountains in Georgia.

'This gathering is for healers looking for spiritual guidance on matters causing suffering on Earth right now. They will be discussing what can be done to cope with the situation and make life better for mankind.'

Lily nodded excitedly. Any chance to see Joan again would be a boon.

'Yes, please!'

Sister Miriam took Lily's hand and in a blink of an eye they found themselves sat in the monastery.

The circular room had grey stone walls with an open roof through which the overhead sunlight streamed through. On stone benches men and women of varying ages, sat silently. Joan was seated on an elevated bench dressed in her usual white gown. Her smiling face glowed as though lit from the inside, complementing the sun's rays gently caressing her skin.

Through the windows, Lily could see rugged steep mountains. She felt humbled as she looked out over the vastness of the landscape. A gentle breeze blew through the windows cooling the room.

Sister Miriam beckoned Lily to sit in front of Joan almost at her feet.

Joan smiled at her in recognition and began to speak in firm yet soft tones.

ಌ

Gergeti Trinity Church, Mount Kazbek, Georgia.

Children.

Compassion

The greatest pain and difficulty that parents face on earth is to lose their children during their lifetime. I am here to reassure you that *mothers whose pregnancies do not end with the birth of a living baby or who lose little children should know that their little ones do not suffer.'*

'Earth is in turmoil and innocent children are losing their lives. *Pray for children in war-torn areas that they may find comfort and be brought to safety. Know the importance of prayer. It rises up and reaches the angels so long as it is from the heart.*

'Souls who are sent suddenly to Spirit are loved and cared for. Children are welcomed with even greater care and tenderness.

'Greater love is always received from those in Spirit, from guides, members of our families who have passed as well as loved ones we've known.'

Lake Sevan, Armenia.

Joy.

Set yourself free.

You ask me how people in power on Earth; politicians, and big corporations, control and manipulate the population.'

Joan looked out over the sea of heads, pausing as though to connect with her inspiration and taking a deep breath before continuing.

'My dear children let me tell you that groups of people, dark forces, have come to the Earth to disrupt the status quo and put hate and fear in your hearts. Have no part in it. Send light to these groups.

'People on Earth were not meant to suffer but to be joyful. But we have brought suffering upon ourselves by our deeds from long ago and by karmic law, we must face what we've done.

'Set yourselves free from the boxes you have built around yourselves and realise what power for good you possess by praying and being positive. Break away from the chains that bind the soul.'

Elephantine Island, Aswan, Egypt.

Golden Age.

Adversity.

Send out light to cleanse our Earth and to the planets *that surround it. This will join the protective light encircling our planet from angelic forces.*

'The negativity of Earth has affected other planets, many of which have a beneficial influence on our planet.

'Saturn sent to Earth law and order, Venus love, and Sirius, the planet of knowledge, sent teachers. Various planets send us rays of coloured light.

'This light pushes away negative conditions that threaten us. The sending out of light is a most serious request if we wish to see a better world for our children and their children. Do not leave a toxic heritage for future generations.

'Spirits throughout the Universe have been working to clear darkness from our planet. Be aware of the importance to us of planets that surround us. Some beings from other planets are too pure to draw close to Earth.

'A Golden Age of spiritual enlightenment is waiting to come in as old energies and negative conditions are cleared and new energies are birthed. Like everything on Earth, there's destruction and a rebirth. And also, for Earth itself.'

Lake Bled, Slovenia.

Spirit Aid.

Prayers.

W*hen you need help, you have only to send out thoughts to your guides or to archangels. Your call will always be answered. Those in Spirit do not interfere in our lives unbidden, you must ask for their help.*

'Pray with all your might for peace and happiness on Earth, for an end to division, violence and hatred. If you have faith, vibrations from your prayers have greater power.

'Be aware of the existence of your lower self. It is ever-present and its greatest joy is to instil fear, negativity and doubt. Look out for this. Recognise this and deny it access, keeping all thoughts positive. Ask Spirit for help and to give you courage.

'When you feel fear and need strength, imagine a six-pointed star above you. Three points point to the heavens and three points down to you. Imagine them bringing light to strengthen and lift you.'

'Learn patience. Spiritual achievements must be worked for and are not gained in your time but in spirit's time.'

Isle of Bute, Scotland.

16. JOAN'S SILVER LININGS.

Optimism.

In thoughts and emotions.

B*e in control of your thoughts and emotions. Put 'self' to one side. Be aware of your thoughts as they occur and make sure they're not negative. Examine your thought patterns - old ways of thinking can creep back in when you thought you had got rid of them. Ask yourself why certain things make you angry, resentful or upset and you'll find the answer. Have the courage to examine difficult events from way back in your life.*

Do you need to forgive others or yourself to let go of them? Have you learnt from the lessons they presented? Or are old feelings holding back your development? Ask for help from your guides, your inner self, and Spirit to cultivate an optimistic attitude.'

'Be in the aura of love and peace each day. Walk with Spirit. Give love to those around you, give a smile, give help, give a kind thought.'

Paddington Canal, London.

Free Will.

Exercise your power.

Know that you have free will to use to help you rise up or sink down. Know when your free will is leading you to do good and drawing you closer to your higher self.

'Learn from the lessons at this Earth school. They're opportunities for you to rise higher and become stronger. You volunteered to come to the earth to learn and each lesson learnt makes you stronger.'

Know that you have free will to use to help you rise up or sink down

Lorgues, France.

Humility

Learn tolerance.

L earn humility, tolerance and love and put right your negative feelings. It is far better to do this while on Earth.

'Lift yourself into the light and let the light be within you and become more pure.

'You are never alone. Your guides are always with you. Do not fear loneliness - in moments of solitude you can be filled with the grace of the Divine.'

છે

'Learn humility, tolerance and love and put right your negative feelings.'

છે

Assisi Courtyard, Umbria, Italy.

Vision.

The gift of Imagination.

Spirit's able to contact you through your imagination, through pictures, words and symbols. Use your imagination to build a picture of the world or personal situation as you would wish it to be. Draw from the imagination the power to overcome obstacles. Use the imagination to open the doors of your mind. Go to the stars, the moon, raise yourself upward.

'Your body's fashioned according to the elements available within the earth Beings from other planets draw similarly from the elements available to them, which are different. Do not call them aliens. They, too, have the holy spirit within. They, too, come to the earth to learn and also to teach.

'Our Divine, the Great Energy of All, wants those on earth to rise up in Spirit, to live on a higher plane of thought. You are Spirit - simply Spirit encased in a body. You forget this, forget who you are.

'Because of the change that is to come over our planet, the vibrations of love and light being sent by an armada in Spirit are more powerful than ever. Have faith that all will be well.'

Joan paused for a moment and smiled as if saying that her teachings for that day had come to an end. She stood up from her bench; turned to Sister Miriam and gave her a gentle embrace 'I'll continue on my travels and leave Lily in your good hands.' With those words, Joan vanished.

❦

Experience is the bridge between knowledge and wisdom.

Morning star, Tuscany, Italy.

17. LOVE.

Service.

Peace of mind and peace for all mankind.

Now it's your time to serve Spirit in helping humanity. This was the reason for your path on Earth in this incarnation. Lily, my dear,' whispered Sister Miriam 'this is one of the reasons I came to help guide you to serve and spread peace to others.

'It is important to help instigate this change even before souls, enter the Earth plane.

'Can I visit the school and see souls preparing to come to Earth?'

Sister Miriam gave a faint nod and reached for Lily's hand.

Lily found herself on a cloud in the glow of the early morning sunrise. Surrounded by sparks of flickering light from a lone morning star illuminating hundreds of happy children.

Lily's heart skipped a beat as she caught a glimpse of a girl with golden hair. Was her Ruby among those preparing to re-enter the earth plane?

'We're all infinite souls, like them, in finite human bodies,' said Sister Miriam.

'Children's purpose on Earth is to teach the true essence of love that's been lost. Love's been twisted out of recognition to be repackaged as a transaction or control.

'We're sent to Earth to acquire wisdom through humility, bravery, sacrifice, patience, kindness and generosity.

'These new souls' experience will be the bridge between knowledge and wisdom.'

Ljubljana, Slovenia.

Intuition.

Connect to your truth.

Sister Miriam, please tell me more about my inner voice. I hear it faintly and yet it is not a sound – more like a soundless voice speaking through my heart.'

There was a long pause then Sister Miriam spoke but not in words through Lily's inner voice.

'This is the voice of your soul speaking. It shares the knowledge and wisdom of your past lives from different realms, from your heart. This knowledge helps you to learn lessons in the present and progress to your future. As you sit in silence and listen, it speaks the truth of your existence.'

Like a flowing river, Sister Miriam continued wordlessly.

'Hear your inner voice and listen to the words. Allow them to speak your truth, without fear, distraction or reaction. Listen in complete acceptance and love to your deepest wisdom.'

'When our minds relate every encounter to previous experiences and make sense with a rational analysis, it reduces our capacity to embrace novel thoughts and ideas.

'When we meditate, we create a capacity to receive wisdom intuitively, without the filter and censorship of the mind. This is known as your inner voice.'

Lily sat for a while letting her words percolate through her body. An electrical charge of knowing ran through her gut. She knew with certainty that she was ready to let go of her desire for her daughter on Earth. She recalled Joan's school and understood her daughter had her journey, as she had hers. They'd always be bonded but her attachment to her was keeping her stuck at the point of her death. And there was no end, just a new beginning.

Love is a state of being.

West London, England

Wisdom.

Wisdom is Love.

L ily, discover your wisdom.

'Journey inside yourself to the bottomless well of love and peace where wisdom lies. This place is Spirit's gift to you, that you brought when you asked to be on Earth during these challenging times. This is the gift we want to remind you of, the place where all is well.'

Another jolt of electricity resonated the truth of Sister Miriam's words in Lily's body.

And the faint voice inside her came through louder this time, clear and powerful.

'What then is love?
Love is the deepest wisdom.
And wisdom is love
Love is a state of being.

'Love is not taking.
Become love itself.
Every thought,
Intention,
Action
Is LOVE.'

Like the petals of a flower unfurling toward the light, Lily began to awaken. Words of truth resounded in her soul.

'I'm on my spiritual path. I'm turning a corner.'

Pyramids, Cairo, Egypt.

18. SWEET PARTINGS.

Farewell Sister Miriam.

In your breath I will find you.

Lily felt a rush of cool wind as she passed over the Pyramid complex in Giza. She felt safe and held in Sister Miriam's slipstream.

Then suddenly she found herself back in the pew, where her spirit guide had found her crying, alone and in fear. It felt like a million lifetimes ago. She'd had so many adventures since meeting her spirit guide in the small chapel.

The night sky was pitch black through the stained-glass windows. Her fingers were cold from where they'd been resting on the back of the pew. She blew into her numb hands.

Sister Miriam, who was sat beside her, stood up abruptly, the soundless voice in Lily's gut screamed.

"Don't go…"

'I'm leaving now, Lily. I must continue my journey through different spiritual realms.'

Lily felt a rising panic in her chest.

'But when will I see you again?'

'Trust that when you call, I'll come. And there's always a secret way to reach me.'

'How?' But even as she said it, Lily's inner voice told her the answer. Loud and clear.

'Close your eyes and observe your breath. As you breathe in and out, you'll become aware of the gap between your in and out breath. Focus on that gap. There you'll find nothingness, a deep peace between the breaths.

'Ask, and in that moment and I'll appear. When you feel fear, stress, anger, or any negativity, stop and take a breath. Ask for the glory of the light to envelop you and the power of all that's love to remove those thoughts and feelings.

'In your breath, I'll find you. In your prayers, I'll answer you. And in your devotion, I'll accompany you.'

Sister Miriam paused and took a deep breath.

'I wish for you, what I wish for all humanity, Lily.'

'What do you wish?'

'To know we're all one. The world right now is full of people who've developed so much hate that at times it's impossible for them to be willing, for even a moment, to let love in.

'So much darkness needs to surface, be brought up, looked at, stared at fully in the face and acknowledged.

'A darkness that's been building up for centuries. All evils and sins carried out on the planet must come into the light now.

'We're at a crucial time of consciousness where many are developing at a fast rate but many still wish to stay in the dark or are unable to move into the light.

'Your job is to hold the light, at all times. To pray and spread the light to those trapped in old paradigms. Don't lower your consciousness to the ego's way of arguing and continue the pattern of separation that's caused so much suffering.

'It's incredibly hard. But lightworkers accepted the task to incarnate at this time.

'You must come together by lifting your vibration as much as you can. Imagining peace. Seeing. Feeling. Creating it.

'Since man came to earth there have been wars and suffering. Terrible deeds done by one human to another. But the world is now waking up.

'Many old souls, like me and Joan, are here with you, joining your vibration, sending light and love. No small act of yours will be in vain. No kindness wasted.

'Stay strong to the beautiful light within you and go there for replenishment and strength. It's the only way. The deception of the ego, that wishes to separate us, must end.

'Love must win. You're part of this love, Lily. You're one of our spiritual foot soldiers. You have a job to do. And I'm your support. I'll hold you up. Guide your way. Give you strength, comfort you when you need it. Soothe your brow when your days are long. I will always love you and give you hope to carry on.

'Know yourself. Feel your power. Spread love and kindness until the dark is swallowed up. I love you eternally. Bless you, and all those who do this work.'

With that Sister Miriam reached for Lily's hands and held them firmly between her own.

'I have a last parting gift.'

In one swift gesture, she lifted the veil off her face.

Lily gasped.

Sister Miriam's skin was as smooth and white as marble. Rich locks of hair as red as a rising sun cascaded over her shoulders. But Lily was mesmerised by the flickering images like on a film reel she could see in the liquid pools of her eyes.

In the reflection, she saw herself give birth to her baby daughter. Then saw time passing, her child with the golden curls and emerald eyes growing up alongside her. Her hand in hers, playing at her feet, walking next to her, lying with her while she slept.

'My daughter Ruby,' said Lily in amazement. 'The girl I saw in Joan's school of life.'

Sister Miriam smiled and nodded.

'Your loved ones are always with you, Lily. They're never far away. Your souls are connected through time and space. The past and the future. Your lives entangled forever more. World without end.'

Sister Miriam pulled her veil back over her face.

'It's now time for me to go, dearest Lily. I have been Ruby's guardian in the spirit world but now she's a grown child and I hand your beloved Ruby back to you. She will always be by your side and you'll always find her in the peace between your breath.'

As Lily opened her mouth to speak, Sister Miriam put a finger over her lips then moved swiftly toward the door.

As she opened it, Lily let out a cry of joy. There, on the other side of the threshold was the young child she'd seen with a face as familiar to her as her own. A girl with golden hair and emerald eyes, smiling at her. RUBY! As Lily drank in the sight of her child, the last iron band of grief snapped around her heart and a love so sweet and tender washed over her. Then Sister Miriam and the young girl faded to nothingness, and all she was left with was the burning love in her heart.

GUIDED MEDITATIONS
AND AN AFFIRMATION.

The Temple of Philae, Aswan, Egypt.

Feroze's Guided Meditation.

What is reality?

Reality is our version of the world played out inside our heads. We each see the world differently depending upon the state of our mind.

It is played out, not in the past or the future but moment by moment. Each moment is separate but joined together like a train moving along tracks giving us the false perception of continuity.

We perceive the world with our senses.

So, how do we see?

Our eyes are like cameras taking snapshots of the world around us. Light is reflected from an object through the cornea, a transparent window at the front of the eye. It is then focused by our lens onto the retina where the light-sensing receptors convert light into electrical impulses. Our brains turn these electrical impulses into meaning; recognising colour, shapes, objects, where they are, how fast they're moving.

These sensations are transmitted through electronic signals that our mind interprets such as colours, tastes, and smells. What and how we experience things, depends upon the quality of our mind machinery at that time.

Each of us perceives the world differently depending upon the state of our mind.

We experience the world as a perceived reality ... an illusion.

Meditation

What is meditation?

There is the world outside. And our perception of that world inside.

The great Sufi poet Rumi once said: "Yesterday I was clever, I wanted to change the world. Today I am wise, I wish to change myself."

Meditation is about changing ourselves from the 'inside out.' It is about creating a purity and focus of the mind by fine-tuning our senses so that we're awakened to see more than the eyes can see.

We perceive the world outside through our senses. Let us call our senses our Five Gates – of taste, touch, hearing, smell, sight and the sixth our mind cognition (our thoughts and feelings).

Imagine that our mind is like a jar of water with mud. If we keep it still the mud will settle and we can see clearly.

To create this clarity of mind we need to focus on any one gate so the others become still and less reactive to our preconditioned mind. Our mind is constantly in flux responding to events happening around us instead of focusing on the moment, acting rationally and objectively to events. Our aim is to be in a state of calm evaluation, observing and acting rationally in the moment.

So, how do we focus on any of the gates? For example, hearing. When we listen to a sound, such as a bell, we connect with the sound and remain connected as the sound resonates and lose that connection when it stops. So, we need to ring that bell again.

We can focus on the flickering flame of a lighted candle using our sight gate and when distracted bring our attention back to the flame.

Focusing on our 'in and out breath', we can keep our connection to the touch gate. When we lose focus with a thought, we can bring our awareness back to the breath again, going in and out of our nostrils.

1. Simple Breath meditation (Anapanna).

This purifies the mind using the power of our breath to remain in the present. By focusing on our sense of touch the other gates rest to create space and capacity in the mind, that's usually in flux with thoughts of our past and fears about our future. Connect with your breath to keep that connection stable and calm.

Ultimately, the aim is to teach the mind to become aware and remain in this awareness zone all the time in whatever we are doing; listening to music, working, watching the sunset, eating etc. In this way, life is much more efficient and richer.

Practice Anapanna Meditation

Take a deep breath.

Let your breath out and release all negative emotions.

Take another deep breath and let it out once more.
Imagine holding a white dove in your hands. Release this bird and as you let it go, know you're giving yourself freedom from past resentments and negative emotions. Buddha once said, "Holding on to resentments is like drinking poison and expecting the other person to die". Make an intention not to harm yourself.

Now gently bring your awareness to your breath. Notice if it is short or long, relaxed and calm. Breathe naturally. Simply observe.

Follow your breath as it comes in and out of your nose, through your nostrils. Feel the sensation, noticing the breath that keeps you alive.

The key is to connect with your breath and maintain that connection. If you lose your connection and are distracted, bring your focus gently back to your breath and re-connect. Be patient with yourself.

If your mind distracts you with a thought, don't engage, just allow it to drift away like a cloud in the sky. Be kind with your mind. Its job is to make thoughts. Befriend it, then bring your awareness gently back to your breath. Do this for at least five minutes in silence.

ॐ

2. Sufi Heart Meditation.

The Sufis believed that the heart, like the mind, has its own senses that they call subtle senses or 'lata'if'.

This mystical Sufi meditation awakens those subtle inner senses of perception, intuition, spirit and higher consciousness to connect with our world inside. And from our heart, to the creative force of the cosmic energy.

The heart was the nexus or link to the five subtle senses.

1. The top of the head was the chakra (or Latifa) of intuition
2. The centre of the forehead was the sensor of perception
3. The right side of the chest was the spirit
4. The solar plexus was the sense of consciousness
5. The Nexus, the heart

It is now understood that stimulating the heart has the effect of regulating the Vagus nerve which is one of the longest and most complex nerves in the parasympathetic nervous system. Vagus nerve exercises also reduce anxiety and create overall well-being.

Practice Sufi Breath Meditation

Bring your breath awareness to your heart. Feel your heart expand as it takes an in breath and contracts when you breathe out.

Keep your breath relaxed and breathe deep into your heart. Imagine your heart is breathing directly in and directly out.

Visualise your heart as your glowing sun. Radiating light and vibrations throughout your body.

Feel the love and compassion that fills you. Embrace these sensations.

Do this for at least five minutes in silence.

❦

3. Mindfulness – Vipassana.

Once you've mastered a meditation practice to observe the breath in Anapanna meditation, move on to a regular practice with the Vipassana full-body breath meditation. The discipline to hold the focus of your breath is necessary to move to this next stage.

This is a state of being in the moment, where you become alive and awake in the now. For example, when you're lost in the beauty of a beautiful sunset and feel you become it.

This technique can teach you how to be in that zone. It helps strengthen your powers of awareness and observation without the mind reacting to its conditioned past. Instead, it helps harness the mind to a state of calmness applying experience and learnings of the past and acting (not reacting) to the present situation.

The Buddha once said, "awareness and observation are the two wings to fly to liberation". It is important to develop both these attributes as we cannot fly with one wing.

This meditation helps develop the power of observation by staying in the moment.

To understand how not to react with our preconditioned mind, we need to examine how our mind works when an event takes place.

1. Consciousness: This is when we become aware that something is happening around us. For example, a noise, something we see, a smell.

2. Perception: How we work out if what's happening is good, bad, pleasant or unpleasant.

3. Sensations: When we feel bodily sensations, for example, if something we perceive makes us angry, our heart beat faster, our blood pressure goes up, we sweat and our stomach becomes tense.

4. Reaction: Our mind recognises bodily sensations of anger from all its past experiences and reacts with its conditioning and experiences of anger. Often this means that a person acts irrationally and loses sight of what's really happening. One ceases to act calmly and rationally.

Vipassana Meditation Practice.

Let us now explore our entire body for sensations by moving our awareness from the top of our head to the tip of our toes, scanning our entire body.

Start at the top of the head, notice any tingling. Move on to scan your face, notice if there's any tightening in the jaw and so on.

Become aware of different sensations, whether pleasant, unpleasant or neutral.

The key is to observe sensations in a detached way without judgment. Scan, then move on.

With practice, you'll be able to scan up and down quickly in rhythm with your in and out breath.

Silently practice this for a few minutes. Remember: awareness of your breath and equanimity in observing breath are the two wings to fly to liberation.

It's critical that before you take on the practice of full body meditation you've mastered breath meditation - where you learn the first wing of awareness which is the foundation of breath meditation.

As a meditator your body will not create the same sensations of anger and hence your mind will not react in an unconditioned way.

You will still have access to your experience and knowledge but in a rational and focused way. You will be calm and, in the moment, able to deal with the situation properly.

Although I have given you the example of anger our senses are continuously reacting to outside stimuli and although we may not fully appreciate our minds going back and forth, negative to positive, we're never really anchored to the moment of now.

Peace between Breaths Meditation.

How to connect with your spirit guide.

Before you go into meditation, recite this message from Sister Miriam:

'In your breath, I will find you.
In your prayer, I will answer you.
In your devotion, I will accompany you.'

Take a deep breath. Hold for a few seconds.

Let your breath out and release all negative emotions.

Bring your focus to the tip of your nose and be aware of your breath coming in and out. Feel the subtle sensation of your breath as it moves in and out of your nostrils. Simply observe the nature of your breath.

Connect with your breath and maintain that connection. If you lose your connection and become distracted, gently bring your focus back to your breath and re-connect. Be patient with yourself.

If your mind distracts you with a thought, don't engage. Once you accept that your mind's function is to create thoughts, you will find that your distractions fade away.

Continue to be aware of your breath coming in and out.

Observe the gap between your in-breath and out-breath. Stay in this gap slightly longer. There is no tension as you continue to breathe normally. You will notice that your out-breath is just a little longer than your in-breath.

As you enter this gap, it becomes more pronounced, and you are now experiencing nothingness. A place where there is neither life nor death, a place of complete bliss.

As your awareness becomes more nuanced, you can observe even the moment within the moment in the peace between your breath.

Keep breathing with awareness for a few minutes.

Bring your breath awareness to your heart. Breathing in and out of your heart. Feel the heart expand as you breathe in and contract as you breathe out.

You have travelled to your heart from your mind. *There lies peace, love. There you will find answers to anything you need to know. Wisdom. Clarity. Divinity. It all comes from that place.*

Observe the gap between your in-breath and out-breath. Stay in this gap slightly longer.

Keep breathing with awareness for a few minutes.

Ask with a sincere heart, and it is in this gap between your breath where you will connect with your spirit guide.

Have no expectations. The spirit connection will take a form and a way that is unique to you and within your capacity. You will be given what you need and not necessarily what you desire. Have faith and trust, and you will know. You will feel a deep peace and joy in your heart as you connect.

Listen to your heart and you will hear your inner voice speak and guide you on your journey.

Practice this Peace between Breaths Meditation for as long or as often as you like.

છ

Gratitude.

Once finished, bring yourself back to the room. Open your eyes and become aware of your surroundings.

Observe the vibrations of peace and beauty within and you'll begin to connect to the present moment.

Put your hands together in gratitude for peace and compassion you have experienced and give thanks for the privilege of living a life as a human being.

Pienza, Tuscany, Italy.

Sister Miriam's guided meditation

For upliftment and to take you out of your daily routine

'Sit quietly for a little while, calming your breathing and relaxing your body.

'Imagine all stresses melting away and being carried off by a passing cloud. See it fade into the distance until it becomes a speck you can hardly see. Be aware of the sounds around you until they too fade into the distance. Make an effort to relax and soothe your neck and shoulders, tummy and solar plexus, fingers and toes. Feel your body softening as it yields into relaxation.

'Think of a beautiful painting you've seen or imagined. Whether a still life or a figure, flowers or trees, sky or clouds, water or mountains. Anything that stirred your soul.

'Bring your awareness to the vision or painting. As if by magic, find yourself stepping into it. Hear the sounds in the picture. Feel the breeze. Smell the air. Be aware of the beauty around you. The stillness. The colours. The fragrance. Be at one with the painting. Melt into the canvas so that there are no edges between you and the painting.

'Maybe you will be offered some guidance. Some whispering. Some comfort. Stay still for as long as you wish.

'When you're ready to open your eyes take a look around. Allow your breathing to become deeper. Remember the absolute calm and quiet you have just experienced. As the vision you've created starts to fade, remember you may visit again whenever you wish.

211

'Change your vision or painting to give you what you need at certain times. Perhaps peace and tranquillity, hope and joy, strength and vitality. Dusk or dawn. Light or dark. Such gifts are yours for the taking.

'We hope this short vision will help to bring you peace. Bless you always with peace, hope and love.'

The Great Pyramid, Cairo, Egypt.

Peace Affirmation.

I have always had a deep respect for the wisdom of the unknown and believe it's our duty to show gratitude.

I am amazed by the magnificence of nature on this tiny blue planet and how it fits into this vast universe. This affirmation is meant to express my humility and demonstrate my appreciation for this order.

I wanted this affirmation to be inclusive for everyone, regardless of their beliefs. I hope that it is not just the words themselves but the meaning behind the words that resonate with you if you choose to speak them.'

Affirmation.

'May I be grounded and rooted in the present moment; I call upon the energy of the Earth to provide stability.

'May I cultivate a strong and resilient spirit, Creating a shield of positivity around me.

'May I embrace my inner power and intuition, Repelling any negative influences or energies.

'May I find the courage to face any challenges that come my way, Granting me strength and balance in my journey.

'May my actions align with love and compassion, That I radiate kindness and understanding.

With gratitude and confidence, I affirm my protection,'May this affirmation empower me and bring me peace, Knowing that I am strong and capable,Whilst I navigate through life's challenges.'

Craig Rebuck. The Sylvan Healing Sanctuary.

The Sylvan Healing Sanctuary.

The Sylvan Healing Centre is a registered charity (reg.no.286004). Sylvan's group of healers provides emotional and physical healing both on its own or as a supplement and support to other Complementary and Alternative Medical (CAM) treatments. Each of our healers has trained over a considerable period to ensure that we can offer the best possible care to all clients.

Sylvan's aim is not only to provide the many benefits that healing energy can offer but to work with clients suggesting ways in which they can help to support their health and wellbeing. In addition to energy healing sessions, either in person or remotely, we offer talks on meditation, breathwork discussions and interviews on many other topics – please see our website www.sylvanhealing.org for details.

ॐ

Acknowledgements.

I would like to express my sincere gratitude to my wife, Farida, and my children Nadir and Sumaya, as well as my son-in-law Brian Collins, for their unwavering patience and support.

I also want to extend my thanks to my colleagues at the Sylvan Healing Sanctuary: Michelle Spencer, Cheryl Jacobson, Craig Rebuck, Geoff Rhodes, Pam Melville, Lynne Fisher, Jacky Slater, Sabine Audibert, and Rosalie Owen, for graciously sharing their spiritual experiences.

A special thank you to Kate Delamere for her exceptional work in editing and story development. I also want to acknowledge and thank my dear friend and publisher, Chris Day of Filament Publishing Ltd, for the beautiful design and publication of the book.

I am deeply grateful to Sir Nigel Carrington, Duncan Baird, Sheryl I. Glick, Professor J. Richard Smith, Kate Delamere, Khalid Awan, Jill Furmanovsky, and Sara Troy for providing their insightful reviews on our book.

Lastly, my heartfelt gratitude to my spiritual master, Ustād, for his guidance and wisdom on the spiritual path.

About The Author.

Feroze Dada was born in Karachi and has lived and worked for most of his life in London. He worked in the finance sector and as an entrepreneur helped several media start-up companies. Some 15 years ago, his life changed when he went to Myanmar to visit his wife's family and became deeply involved in working with a Buddhist monastery in Shan Province, helping it to become self-sufficient in looking after 1200 orphaned or abandoned children.

He went on to become a meditation practitioner as well as continued to work with his Sufi teacher, learning how to live a fulfilled and meaningful life by helping others.

He's the interviewer and producer of online TV series Discovering Humanity and Our One World, author of Children of the Revolution; *A Spiritual Journey to Burma and Buddhism* and A Disciple; *The Spiritual Path to Infinite Happiness.*

As well as his work as founder of The Inle Trust Charity www.inletrust.org.uk set up to help children at the Phaya Taung monastery in Myanmar, he teaches and promotes meditation at The Sylvan Healing Sanctuary in London, a community of healers and teachers that offer energy healing, meditation and mindfulness.

His wife MuMu (Farida) is from Taunggyi, Myanmar. They have two children; Nadir and Sumaya, and grandchildren Layla and Rafferty. They divide their time between their homes in London and Italy.

THE END